ROYAL LEAMINGTON SPA

Images

From the Past

ROYAL LEAMINGTON SPA

Images
From the Past

W.G. Gibbons

JONES - SANDS PUBLISHING

First Published in Great Britain by
Jones-Sands Publishing 1995

ISBN 0-947764-86-0

To preserve the quality and character, the pictures in this publication
have not been retouched in any way.

This book was designed by:-

Jones-Sands Publishing
Upton
Wirral
L49 6PQ
England
Tele/Fax (0151 606 0240)

Typeset in Great Britain by Jones-Sands Publishing
Printed by Clifford Press Ltd, Coventry
Marketed and distributed by Jones-Sands Publishing

AUTHOR'S ACKNOWLEDGEMENTS

Most of the illustrations come from my own collection but I am most grateful to the following whose valuable photographs are
here reproduced.

Mr. G. Abbotts, Mr. G.E. Archer, Mrs. H. Arnold, Automotive Products PLC., Mr. J. Baldwin, Miss J.A. Bates, Mr. D. Bicknell,
Mr. D Billings, Birmingham Central Library, Mrs. E. Cater, Mr. P. Chater, Mr. F. Chew, Mr. Churchill, City of Coventry Local Studies
Library, Mr. R. Collingridge, Mr. J.A.G. Coltas, Mr. F. Cooper, Mrs. C. Dark, Mr. A.G.S. Davies, Mrs. M. Deeming, Mrs. W. Edwards,
Sidney Flavel PLC., Mrs. E. Fletcher, Mrs. M. French, Mr. J.G. Gardner, Mr. J. Gaskins, Mrs J. Hawkins, Mr. P.V. Hewitt, Mr. B.
Hickman, Mrs E. Hitchcox, Mr. G. Jerrim, Mrs. I. Jones, Leamington Spa Courier, Leamington and Warwick Evening Telegraph, Mr.
R. Lines, Loft Theatre, Mrs. M. Lofts, Mrs L. Mayhew, Mrs. H. Meades, Mrs. J. Mills, Mrs. J. Morris, Mr. J. Neville, Mr. J.A.
Newstead, Post Office, Sid and Joy Savage, Mrs. H. Scott, Mr. L. Simmons, Mrs. M. Simmons, Mrs. J. Strevens, Mrs, J. Sumner, Mr.
A Sturgess, Mr. A. Thacker, The Autocar, A. Tomes Ltd., Mr. C. Ward, Mrs. E. Warr, Warwickshire County Library (at Leamington and
Warwick), Warwick District Council, Warwickshire Museum, Wimbledon Lawn Tennis Museum, Miss A.E. Wright.

Warm thanks are also extended to the following for their willing helpfulness:- Mrs. M. Abbotts, Jill Bailey, Mr. C.D. Baker, Mrs.
Enid Cater, Maureen Davies, Terry Gardner, Jackie Godson, Barry Hickman, Sid Savage, Mr. A. Jennings, Mr. Bob Jones, Mr. A. Peat,
Warwickshire County Record Office, Warwickshire and Worcestershire Life. Also grateful thanks to any others inadvertently omitted.

Illustrations: Cover: *Lower Parade about 1925.*
                   Page 1:   *The ladies of Austin Edward's family stroll out from their home* Milverton Lawn, *15 Warwick New Road Leamington.*
                   Page 2:   *Linden Avenue with the Pump Room Gardens on the left and Dormer Place on the right c.1890.*
                   Page 3:   *Fashions in the late 1800's are seen on the New River Walk alongside the lazy Leam.*

CONTENTS

Town Growth

Social Life

Signs of the Past

On the Move

Letter and the Law

TOWN GROWTH

Introduction

Unlike ancient places such as Warwick and Coventry, Leamington is a comparatively young town. Therefore, apart from the old village, the stages of its 200 year progress can today be identified without much difficulty. In the early days of the Spa there were, in effect, two separate towns - the original old one to the South of the River Leam and the splendid new town to the North. Even today the original division between the two areas is clearly defined by the river and the adjacent green belt of the Jephson and Pump Room Gardens.

Much of the old town still retains its early street plan and buildings so that the growth there can easily be traced. Likewise the grand new town remains, despite many regrettable losses, an attractive example of 19th century planning for our study and enjoyment.

From 1860 onwards expansion steadily continued; land on the outskirts being gradually occupied by more and more houses. The Victorian painted-stucco villa, the long Edwardian terraced street, the 1930's upper-class mansions lining the chestnut avenue and the council estates, built before and after War II, each in their own way mark for us the differing stages in the growth of the town. Over the years the combined activities of the local authority and private enterprise have produced a place of fascinating diversity.

(Left) A peaceful summer scene captured by famous Victorian photographer Francis Bedford c.1870. The lovely avenue in Holly Walk leads down to the buildings in Regent Grove and Clarendon Street with Hamilton Terrace on the left.

The Hamlet of Leamington Priors

There appears to have been a settlement of some kind on the low south bank of the River Leam at least as early as the 7th century. The Domesday Book (1086) records details of "Lamintone" and from 1166 to 1539 it was owned by the Priors of Kenilworth during which time it's title became Leamington Priors.

Over the centuries there was little growth; in 1663 there were but 46 dwellings while in 1800 there were still possibly no more than 50 (when the population was about 300).

The sleepy village of about 1800 consisted of a Manor House, three farms, approximately fifty labourer's cottages, a small church with it's Vicarage, a tiny Post Office, two Inns; the Dog and the Bowling Green, a water mill, a smithy and wheelwright's shop, a Parish Poor House, a market, a set of stocks, a duckpond and last but not least a humble spring of mineral water on waste ground near the church.

Connecting with neighbouring villages of Whitnash and Lillington was an ancient lane (its line can still be traced today) and, leading to Warwick and Southam, was the rutted London Road (which became High Street where the road passed through the town).

All Saints Church and cottages, 1822.

*No. 15 and 17 Church Street, 1974. Two of Leamington's oldest cottages:
basically timber-framed and originally thatched.*

DEVELOPMENT: The Old Town (1790-1840)

The success of the Spa was due to the presence of the mineral springs combined with the commercial zeal of two local tradesmen - cobbler Benjamin Satchwell and his crony, inn-keeper William Abbotts, who both emerged from rural obscurity to become founders of the fashionable Spa town. For several years they strove to find a way of exploiting the medicinal properties of the waters and thus bring prosperity and fame to Leamington. Their efforts were rewarded in 1784 when the pair discovered the village's second spring on Abbotts' land in Bath Lane and ultimately, to paraphrase the words of Nathaniel Hawthorne "out of this muddy ditch gushed out, as if by magic, a multitude of fine new buildings of every kind". Following the opening of Abbotts' *Original Baths* in 1786 the curative powers of the saline waters were soon recognized and generally advertised – thus began the ever-increasing flood of wealthy visitors to the Spa. From about 1790 the town steadily established itself in its new role; indications of a boom town abounded with an air of excitement, enthusiasm and optimism that continually stimulated everyone to think up new plans of every sort.

The initial momentum however was soon halted and for about a decade there was little progress. The dormant period of 1793-1806 was mainly due to the national financial burden of

Houses in Satchwell Place, 1981. Were Hopton's Boarding House (1810), restored 1979-81.

the war with France coupled with a disastrous harvest of 1799. Future prospects appeared grim; a guide book of the time tells us "In Bath Lane (Bath Street) there are but two buildings; the New Inn and Abbotts' Baths, then a gaping space between these and Wise's Baths in High Street. The Lane is rough and unprepared, deep cart ruts in the middle with hedges on each side, an open dike on the East - all in unmerited neglect and silence".

The halt in development was but a temporary matter as between 1806 and 1820 there was a great renewal of enterprise and activity. Changes to the humble village now took place rapidly, the pattern being similar to those in most ancient towns where new buildings intermingled with, or replaced, the old and new streets extended to the outskirts. At this time Leamington had a strange mixture of thatched cottages and new brick-built houses.

Most of the growth was in the Bath Street/High Street area. Clemens and Gloucester Streets were commenced in 1808, followed shortly after by houses in Church Street (1825) and Wise Street. Brunswick Street, an extension of Clemens Street, was started in 1827. The main buildings were as follows:- in the Bath Street area (including present Victoria Terrace): Abbotts' Baths (1786); the New Inn (1793); Lord Aylesford's Well, over the original spring, (1803); Robbins' Baths (1806); the Theatre (1813); Waterloo House (1818); the Parthenon Lower Assembly Rooms (1821); Victoria Terrace (1838); the Post Office (1846) and Victoria Pavilion. In High Street were Wise's Baths (1790); Read's Baths (1806); Albion Hotel (1813); James Bisset's Paragon Museum and Art Gallery (1819); Copps' Royal Hotel (1827); the Town Hall (1831) and Warneford Hospital and Bathing Institution (1834). In Clemens Street appeared Smart's Baths (1816/17), Bisset's Picture Gallery, Fairweather's Fumigating

(continued page 15)

Bath Street, Bath Hotel, Theatre, Abbotts' Baths, 1822.

First Town Hall (1831), High Street, 1982. Now Polish Club.

(below) Spencer Street, Parish Church and Aylesford Well, about 1890.

Bath Street and Victoria Terrace, about 1905.

Aylesford Well and Parish Church, about 1890.

Victoria Terrace, about 1910.

Baths, a theatre (1849) and the Oxford (1812) and Orange Hotels.

Further developments were Hopton's Boarding House, Satchwell Place (1810) the establishment of Ranelagh Pleasure Gardens (present Flavel's site) (1811), erection of Shrubland Hall (1822) and the setting up of a second market in Abbotts Street (1825). The building of a grand block of terraced houses (Eastnor Terrace), was commenced in Old Warwick Road in 1837 but was never completed.

(New Town) Union Parade, Bedford Hotel & Regent Hotel, 1822. At this stage buildings extended Northwards only just beyond Regent Street.

Growth in the old town was finally brought to an end by about 1830 as the new town had by that time become well established. A rapid slump took place south of the river and sadly became very much a ghost town of empty hotels and defunct Baths with an overall atmosphere of depression and neglect.

The New Town (1810-1840)

The concept of a new town for Leamington is clearly described in the following words from Moncrieff's Guide of 1830, "In the year 1806 some spirited speculators, tired of planning improvements in the old town, determined to found a new one. For this noble and venturous undertaking, that part of Leamington on the North bank of the river, rising from the Leam, on a gradual and charming ascent, consisting chiefly of the grounds of the late Bertie Greatheed Esq., was selected as the most advantageous spot". This bold decision was prompted mainly by problems of land purchase in the village area. For about 20 years following the opening of Abbotts' Baths, landowners were reluctant to sell quickly, one reason being that some of them preferred to hold back and sell slowly on a rising market.

Holly Walk with Hamilton Terrace, about 1900.

By 1810 the town's Improvement Commissioners had formulated an overall plan for the new town and this was roughly in the shape of a square with Warwick Street as it's northerly limit. Starting from scratch there was complete freedom to lay out a gridiron plan of streets, terraces, squares and crescents. This was to have the main street, the Parade, as the central 'spine' with two broad 'ribs' – Cross Street (Regent Street) and Warwick Street intersecting it at right angles. Quite a number of side streets, East and West of the Parade, were included in the scheme. The heart of the new town was to be midway along the slope of the Parade - around the Regent Street area.

The first house was erected in 1808 on the corner of Regent Street and the Parade, followed in 1810 by a range of 20 terraced houses running southwards from Woodward's present site on the Parade.

In spite of the initial rush to purchase land the actual growth was rather spasmodic, with buildings erected here and there in a somewhat piecemeal fashion. Fortunately construction closely conformed to a regulated order and style rather than of individual design, so that eventually a town of unified streets and terraced houses emerged.

By 1830 there were 1100 houses in 111 streets and the population was about 6,000. Four years later a tremendous amount of building had taken place and planned growth had already overtaken the earlier northern limit of Warwick Street in the form of the Upper Parade,

(continued page 24)

Euston Place, about 1905.

(above) Lower Parade, about 1890.

(right) Upper Parade, about 1890.

THE ONLY
MANUFACTORY
FOR THE
GENUINE
LEAMINGTON
SALTS.

A striking absence of traffic in Bath Street early one summer's morning about 1895. First on the right stand the premises of Chemist James Spilsbury and the birthplace of his famous son Sir Bernard Spilsbury. Next we see on the other corner of Regent Place, the haven of all T.T. travellers, the Westminster Temperance Hotel and Coffee Tavern. The porch on the left belongs to the Royal Music Hall and the well-known Lower Assembly Rooms.

(above) Waterloo Place and Clarence Terrace with St. Alban's Church, 1880's.

(left) Clarendon Square, 1956.

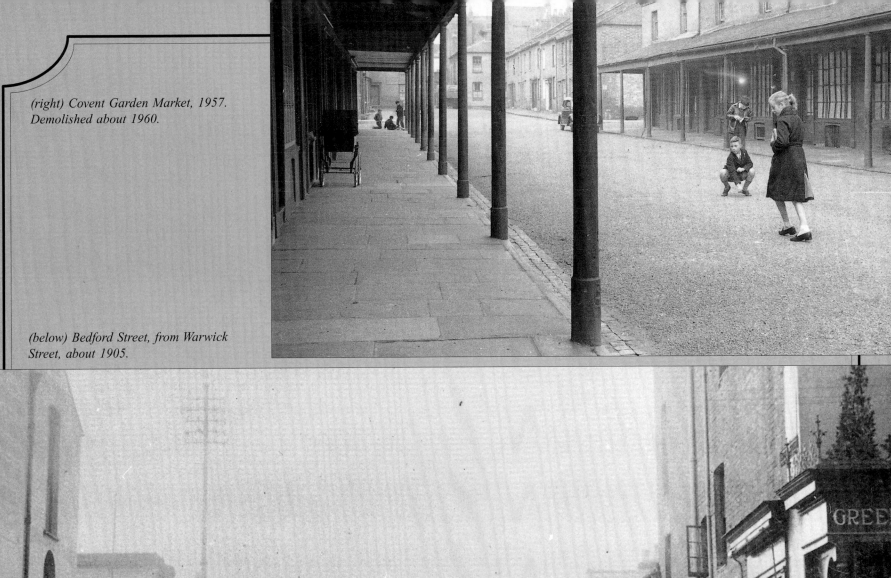

(right) Covent Garden Market, 1957.
Demolished about 1960.

(below) Bedford Street, from Warwick
Street, about 1905.

John Street, 1956. Demolished same year.

South Parade (Clarendon Avenue), Beauchamp and Binswood Avenues and, by 1840, the 19th century town we see today was virtually completed.

To the West of the Parade there was Warwick Street, Waterloo Place, Clarence Terrace, Clarendon Square, Portland Street, Dale Street, Grove Street, Portland Place and an extended Regent Street, while to the East of the Parade stood Warwick Street, Lansdowne Crescent and Circus, Regent Street, Newbold Terrace and Hamilton Terrace. Most of the public buildings were of course on the Parade; they were the Royal Pump Room and Baths (1814), the Bedford Hotel (1811), Upper Assembly Rooms (1812), the Regent Hotel (1819), the Lansdowne, Imperial and Clarendon Hotels (all about 1832). Elsewhere in the town were the Golden Lion and Angel Hotels in Regent Street (both about 1810). In Warwick Street there was Dr. H. Jephson's residence, Beech Lawn (1832). At a later time also appeared the Leamington Tennis Court, Bedford Street (1846).

Windsor Street, 1971. Demolished about 1972.

Brook Street, 1954.
Demolished same year.

King Street, about 1905.

Parish Church and Pump Room about 1910.

During the period 1835 - 1869 further housing development took place in Avenue Road, and in the areas of King/ Queen Street and Union Road/Hyde Place.

The new town was not to be without it's attractive natural features: in 1843 Dr. John Hitchman instituted a scheme for the laying out of many lovely avenues while, in 1846, the now-famous Jephson Gardens were opened.

As expansion occurred on both sides of the river it became vital that there were adequate crossings to link the two districts. The main "Leamington" Bridge (later named "Victoria") was built in 1809; being extended in 1840 and 1848, then followed the erection of Willes Bridge (1827) and Adelaide Bridge (1850 version).

The general impression of the bright new Spa is of a spacious, beautiful town with wide, well planned roads and grand terraces, crescents and squares. This indeed was true as regards the fashionable main streets and open spaces but understandably no contemporary guide book mentions that behind the palatial houses were large areas of disease-ridden slums of unbelievable filth and squalor. Here were the dwellings for the large numbers of working people. The smallest of houses, gloomy narrow streets, alleys, courts and yards made up the seamy side of Leamington; an aspect which escaped the notice of it's wealthy and privileged visitors. To a degree it can be accepted that the old village would have a fair measure of slum property but, considering that the 'other' town, North of the river, was an entirely new development, it is difficult to understand how such shocking conditions were also allowed to appear there.

THE LATE VICTORIAN TOWN

The popularity of Leamington as a fashionable watering place rapidly waned after the extensive introduction of the railways in the 1850's made it easy for high society to indulge in the new fad of sea bathing in places such as Brighton.

With it's abundance of fine houses the town then soon became popular as a residential area, attracting large numbers of retired high-ranking officers of the Armed Forces, the Church and the Empire's Civil Service.

As the influx of wealthy visitors dwindled there was a proportionate drop in the number of workers required and because there was virtually no industry in the area, large numbers began to travel daily, mostly by rail, to work in the factories and offices of Coventry, Birmingham and Rugby. In 1852 the Local Board of Health was established and up to 1875 it carried out very useful schemes such as the founding of a Public Library at the old Town Hall, High Street (1857), the purchase of the Pump Room and Baths with adjoining Gardens (1868) and extensive improvement to the river and sanitation.

Borough status was granted in 1875 and in 1890 the urban parts of Milverton and Lillington were incorporated into the Borough - despite fierce opposition from the 'upper-

The Parade, about 1935.

crust' residents of these districts who had no wish to be linked with the scorned tradespeople of Leamington.

Most building work was carried out during the 1870 - 1900 period when many substantial dwellings appeared in Warwick New Road, York Road, Priory Terrace, Upper Holly Walk and at the east end of Lillington Avenue. Smaller but attractive terraced houses were erected in St. Mary's Road, Victoria Street and Road - each house usually having it's own small front garden and a larger one at the rear.

Services to the public were greatly enhanced by the erection of the following: The Public Hall, Windsor Street (1854), the Arboretum Hydropathic Establishment, Tachbrook Road (1863), the General Post Office, Priory Terrace (1870), the Theatre Royal, Regent Grove

Willes Road, about 1905.

Warwick Street, about 1910.

(1882), the new Town Hall, Parade (1884), Denby Buildings and Liberal Club, Regent Grove (1885) and the Pump Room Public Swimming Bath (1890). The Parish Church was extended by the addition of two bays to the nave and a western bell tower (1898-1902), while the Warneford Hospital had, by 1900, doubled it's size by the erection of two large wings. Many amenities were also improved: these were the New River Walk and a Weir (1862) – in the present Princes Drive area, new waterworks – at Campion Terrace (1879) and at Lillington (1900), York Walk and Bridge (1893), Victoria Park (1897), Eagle Recreation Ground (1899) and a new weir at the Mill (1899-1902). Illumination of the streets by electricity was first tried out in 1887. From 1851 to 1901 records state that the population had increased from nearly 16,000 to about 27,000 and consequently one would assume that there had been an appropriate increase in the number of houses. In fact the number of new dwellings built was very small and the large population figure given by the 1901 Census was mainly due to the 1890 inclusion of Milverton and Lillington in the Borough boundary.

Lansdowne Crescent, about 1905.

Heath Terrace, 1969.

House at No. 6 Wood Street, 1980.

Cubbington Road, Lillington, about 1950.

After the decline of the Spa no doubt large numbers of workers left the town and by so doing there would have been enough working-class housing available for many years to come.

THE TWENTIETH CENTURY TOWN

Despite a fall of 200 in the population between 1891 and 1911, the average growth rate of the population for the period 1891-1939 was quite steady although not as rapid as in previous years.

Between 1890 and 1918 a number of terraced houses were erected. These were in Villiers Street, North Villiers Street, Rugby Road (North West side), Gaveston and Strathearn Road, York Road and in the areas of Wathen Road/Campion Road, Shrubland Street, Court Street/Althorpe Street. Several much-needed housing estates were constructed in the 20 years 1919 - 1939 namely at Shrubland, Rushmore, the Holt, Lillington and in the Baker Avenue/Cashmore Avenue area. Stud Farm and Manor Farm estates were commenced at this time. Other houses were built in Northumberland and Woodcote Roads, Rugby Road (West end), Radford Road (East end), Leicester Street and Windmill Road.

In the late 1930's there were large numbers of old, big houses to let or for sale and, in spite of very low prices, many remained empty for years, giving a rather sad appearance to the respective districts. Bad housing conditions in a lot of the older properties and an insufficient supply of good-standard houses of popular sizes tended to impede a change to a more lively and prosperous population.

(left) Warwick Place about 1880.

Denby Buildings, Regent Grove and the Town Hall about 1920.

From 1945 to 1965 the population had increased by 11,000 and consequently from 1950 onwards there was a great deal of new housing development. This was massive expansion to the existing estates of Stud Farm and Manor Farm, the three new estates of Beverley Hills, Sydenham and Queensway and also on the site of the old Campion Road Brickworks.

Changes also took place in or near the town centre with the demolition of some older properties such as in Windsor Street, John Street, Brook Street and the areas of Park Street/Chandos Street/King Street/Queen Street. Often the result has been the creation of bleak car parks but fortunately there are also instances where the vacant plots have been occupied again by attractive new dwellings. Another gradual change has been that in areas such as Kenilworth Road, Lillington Avenue, Holly Walk and Newbold Terrace many of the larger houses, often over a century old, have either been converted into flats or replaced by new buildings.

General improvements and public buildings included the construction of the Mill Suspension Bridge with the adjoining Mill Gardens (1903), the Free Library, Technical and Art School, Avenue Road (1902), Urquhart Hall (1905), Jephson Gardens riverside Bandstand - later Pavilion (1909), Princes Drive Bridge (1923), Bath Cinema (1925), Bath Assembly Rooms (1926), Public Art Gallery and Museum, Avenue Road (1928), Regal Cinema (1931), Branch Public Libraries at Valley Road, Lillington (1960) and at Shrubland Street (1964), Edmondscote Sports Track (about 1960), the Spa Centre (1972) and the Newbold Comyn Recreation Ground (first phase 1973).

Harrington House, Newbold Terrace, built 1869, demolished 1967.

A mid-morning view about 1890, of a sun-lit Parade looking strangely empty of people and traffic. At the top, the clock tower of Christ Church makes a splendid focal point and outside the cluttered window of the Bedford Stores, a charming little donkey with his cart, waits meekly for his master to return.

A deserted Upper Parade about 1910 with the well-known Christ Church at the far end. Making a fine focal point, the church was built in 1825 and demolished in 1959. The grand Clarendon Hotel, on the far right, was opened in 1832 and finally closed in 1983 – to be converted into offices a few years later.
On the far left were the premises of Stevenson and Sons, carriage builders, and at No. 6 and No. 8, the studios of photographer Robert L. Graham.

SOCIAL LIFE

Introduction

The new Spa town in the period 1820 to 1850 had two levels of society. There were the wealthy and powerful visitors and, separated by a huge gulf, the greatly under-privileged masses of the working classes.

The town's popularity as a Spa declined between 1850 and 1900 becoming more a place of permanent residence and attracted large numbers of retired, high-ranking members of the Armed Services, the Church and also from the Empire. It likewise attracted professional men as the coming of the railways enabled them to live in Leamington and travel each day to Birmingham, Coventry and even London for business.

From about 1900 up to the 1930's the character of the town changed again and earned the title of "poor, proud and pretty". Many of its grand houses stood empty and neglected as the retired Generals, Bishops etc. died or were forced, by financial embarrassment, to move to less sumptuous accommodation. Thus began the final change when Leamington became the home of the middle and working classes and today the old social distinctions have to a great extent disappeared.

A shy young lady shades her eyes from the summer morning sun at the porch of "The Cottage" at the top of Holly Walk, and facing Newbold Comyn Farm, c.1880. The timber-framed building was replaced by an all-brick house c.1890. In the distance the curving road leads up to "Newbold Beeches" house.

PEOPLE AND PLACES

y 1860 the population of the town had reached about 17,000; this figure increasing to about 26,000 by the turn of the century. The population increased further to about 30,000 by the 1930's.

The well-to-do upper classes lived in their fashionable houses situated in the many fine terraces, squares and crescents. Their lives were comfortable and leisurely as, with a cheap and plentiful supply of domestic servants, they could spend much of their time shopping in the smart Parade, strolling through the Jephson and Pump Room Gardens, socialising while partaking of coffee, tea and even the Spa water at the popular Pump Room.

Leamington Spa continued to be a successful inland resort for summer visitors, these staying at large hotels such as the Regent, Clarendon, Manor House and Crown; they also added their numbers to the well-dressed throng whose main aim was to enjoy the delightful amenities of the Spa and surrounding district.

High Street, with Crown Hotel, 1860.

Life in the early 1900's for the working classes was not so easy. Labouring for long hours and poor pay, they had little time or money for leisure and entertainment and their standard of living was indeed low. Their homes were in crowded back-to-back houses in areas

(right) Linden Avenue, Pump Room Gardens, about 1910.

(left) Tea time in the Pump Room, about 1925.

such as Satchwell, Park, Kenilworth, Tavistock, Queen and King Streets - many of these being immediately behind the splendid terraces of the town centre. Conditions for the ordinary folk were not good, yet, by being in high-density housing areas, they were a closely-knit and happy people. The lively community spirit in adversity and in good times has been lost for ever as the old, poor streets have been demolished and the people moved away to new estates on the outskirts of the town. Social life was indeed simple but enjoyed to the full in a strong bond of togetherness.

Pump Room Gardens, about 1910.

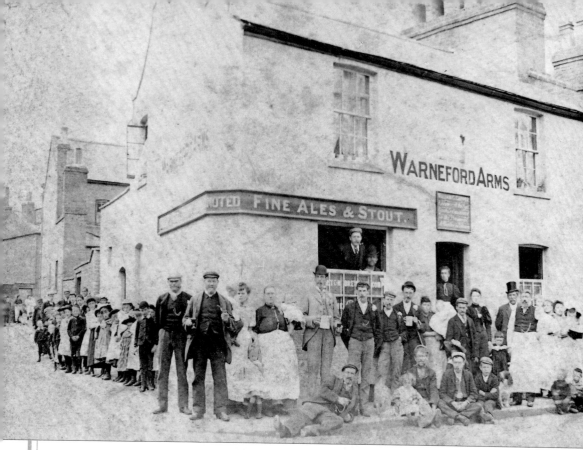

Warneford Arms, Charles Street, about 1890.

(right) Clarence Street. Fire at Flavel's Foundry, Silver Jubilee (K.G.V.) Day, 1935.

King Street, about 1905.

Earning a Living

As the character of the town altered so did the situation for the working classes. The people of the humble village, prior to 1800, were agricultural workers but with the development of the Spa (1810-1840), the main activity was in the building and allied trades. Following the decline in the construction boom the work pattern changed again. The 1851 census listed about 10,000 employed persons, a third of which were domestics, shop assistants, makers of clothes, laundresses and those associated with transport - this small army providing essential services to the fashionable visitors. An 1814 song by James Bisset contains the quaint verse:-

> *There are eminent pastry-cook's shops,*
> *With butchers, and brewers, and bakers,*
> *There are fishmongers, drapers, and tailors'.*
> *But, as yet, there are no undertakers."*

Windmill Inn, Tachbrook Road, about 1917.

Working conditions were grim; hours were long and pay poor. Local householders were advised to keep the number of servants down to a minimum and only employ them for 51 weeks of the year "so that they could not claim Leamington as their permanent residence and therefore would not be chargeable to the actual parish of their birth" i.e. other than Leamington. It is surprising however that in 1851 only four persons were recorded as unemployed. The town then could hardly claim to be industrial as it still had only a handful of tiny works making bicycles and later, motor cycles. Undertakings such as the canal, railway, water, gas, postal and municipal also provided a fair number of jobs. Unfortunately very few pictorial records exist of this early period - certainly very few photographs.

In the early 1900's the availability of cheap labour brought about another occupational change to Leamington. The town began its ever-increasing development as a popular midland shopping centre and also revived its role as an inland resort, thus providing custom for the splendid hotels bequeathed from the Spa era. Others recognised the advantageous

(continued page 54)

The eleven Smith brothers during building of Town Hall, 1882-84.

W. Collins, butcher, 9 Windsor Street, about 1910.

(right) Metcalf's, 1 & 3 Clemens Street, about 1900.

The Maxwell Dyer Orchestra pose for the camera at Bobbby's Restaurant about 1930. Bobby's, at 152-156 Parade, was one of the town's top-class stores and its restaurant was advertised as "the accepted rendezvous where friends meet friends for morning coffee, lunch or tea".
After being occupied by Debenhams for some years, the building was demolished in 1988 and the Regency Arcade was erected on the site.

(left) Three waitresses (Mrs. E. Warr, centre) of Pump Room Balcony Café about 1930.
(below) George ("Nobby") Clarke with his portable knife-grinding machine in Northumberland Road 1957.

(left) Driver, Reg. Lines, with first Bedford Stores motor delivery van (Renault) June 1925.

Sandblasting (left) and fettling (below) shops,
Flavel's Eagle Foundry, 1937.

(right) 3 ton girder being moved
into place during the rebuilding of
GWR station. March 8th 1938.

labour situation and commenced to set up engineering works on the outskirts; in particular Automotive Products and Henry Griffiths (jewel factory) both in Tachbrook Road. The business of Sidney Flavel had continued to expand and now had two foundries, at the Eagle and Imperial works. A brilliant pioneer of the automobile industry was Charles T. Crowden who produced about a dozen light cars at his motor car works, Packington Place, Leamington (1898-1905). One of the cars survives in the Coventry Museum of Road Transport as a permanent reminder of the town's short-lived motor enterprise. Possibly there are still a few Leamingtonians around who remember World War I "shadow factory", at the former roller skating rink in Dormer Place, where aircraft wings were produced.

During the 40-year period 1930-1970 the increased availability of public transport, private cars and motor cycles encouraged large numbers of factory and office workers to seek the higher wages offered in the large industrial and commercial centres lying within a short distance of the town. In Leamington the flourishing factory of Automotive Products increased it's workforce to 7,000 by 1970 thereby making it undoubtedly the largest single employer and a key factor in the fortunes of the town. Since World War II large industrial estates have been constructed in the Queensway, Court Street, Sydenham and Heathcote areas and further employment has been provided by large chain stores, namely Woolworths, Marks and Spencer, Boots, Tesco and Rackhams – all have moved into the fashionable Parade. As Leamington is ideally situated in the heart of England and has a pleasant environment, an ever-increasing number of national firms have established their head offices in the district.

HAVING A GOOD TIME

During the early part of the 1800's, in stark contrast to the luxurious lives of the rich, the poor of Leamington struggled to survive in the most squalid conditions situated in the back streets of both the new and old town. Working six full days a week, to long hours (an eight-hour day was not generally adopted until about 1900), it was only natural that the working classes sought to escape from their slum houses and find relief in whatever entertainment there was within their financial reach and their restricted free time (holidays were almost unknown). Religious meetings were organised everywhere but these were usually forsaken for more earthly pleasures. A happy social atmosphere was readily available on the doorstep in the numerous public houses, inns, taverns, vaults, ale houses and gin palaces. As travel was not feasible the pub was the focal point of community life; each had its clubs,

(Right) Pleasure coaches outside the Regent Hotel about 1900

Theatre Royal, Regent Grove, about 1925.

summer outing fund and other social activities. Most were incurable gamblers and pub raffles were regular events. The rich residents enjoyed more sophisticated pleasures with their hunts, steeplechases, balls, concerts, theatres and use of the parks and gardens (not then public) not forgetting the Pump Room, an important fashionable meeting place where a band played every morning from 8 till 9. The tiny theatre in Bath Street (1813-1833) and the later Theatre Royal, Clemens Street (1849-1866) were not well patronised, even though famous names often appeared on their boards.

From 1900 onwards other exciting and reasonably priced forms of entertainment appeared in the town. Leamington had its share of pioneer moving picture houses. Public film shows before the days of Talkies were first given in makeshift halls as at the Blue Café (Parthenon) and at the ex-theatre in Clemens Street but risk of fire very soon caused their closure. Opening in December 1910 the first proper picture house was the Colonnade Theatre, Victoria Colonnade previously, the Victoria Pavilion. Early sound films such as "Sonny Boy" and "Hells' Angels" captivated large audiences in the early 1920's. 1910 saw the erection of the purpose-built Bedford Street Picture House, later renamed Scala and nicknamed the Bijou or the Fleapit. The Scala advertised itself as the home of "Talking, Singing and Dancing Pictures". Soon it became obvious that moving pictures had come to stay and in 1925 the Bath Cinema, later Clifton, opened in Spencer Street followed in 1931 by the splendid 1930's style Regal picture palace in Augusta Place which had a mighty Barbieri organ. The 1930's were truly the heyday of the cinema as, during the Depression years, people found escape into the unreal but magical world of the Hollywood extravaganzas. Going to the "flicks" in the prewar years became for many almost a way of life. The grand old Theatre Royal, Regent Grove had closed in 1934 and, after conversion, was reopened in 1935 as the cosy Regent Cinema, the fourth in the town. The superb Compton organ delighted audiences during the interval.

In the latter half of the 19th Century the number of wealthy visitors rapidly declined but the upper-class places of entertainment struggled on with dwindling audiences. There was a gradual levelling-out of social distinctions and improved wages enabled more of the underprivileged to enjoy pleasures that previously were beyond their means. Music halls such as that at the Parthenon, Bath Street, offered exuberant magical evenings and smaller assembly rooms became available at the larger inns for public balls. The Golden Lion, Regent Street, the oldest pub in the new town, often held such

(continued page 60)

Scala Cinema, Bedford Street, 1953.

Clifton Cinema, Spencer Street, 1982.

Regal Cinema, Augusta Place, about 1968.

functions when "an efficient quadrille band" or "a celebrated German band" was engaged. Fun fairs, Mops at Warwick and Stratford together with summer outings were all annual highlights while for the more selective there were the numerous clubs and societies which covered subjects like orchestral, choral, dramatic, scientific, sketching, photographic, brass bands, billiards and the usual sports. Free libraries, art galleries and coffee taverns also appeared in the town. Travelling circuses at the Victoria Grand Circus (Pavilion), Victoria Colonnade, and cockfighting were always well supported.

The Colonnade cinema closed about 1934 and became a roller skating rink (1936-1939) and later the site was occupied by the present Loft Theatre. The Scala was demolished in 1954, as was the Regent, ex-Theatre Royal, in 1984. The Clifton ended its career in 1982, the building becoming Lester's entertainment complex in 1983. From the 1920's right up to the 1940's public dances were all the rage; they were held locally at the Blue Café, the Palais de Dance, the Town Hall, the Pump Room, the Masonic Rooms and the Salisbury Hall.

(above) Advertising card, 1862

Queens Arms, Queen Street, about 1910.

Town Hall Dance, about 1925.

Town Band, about 1910.

Jephson Garden's Lake, 1984.

GOING TO CHURCH

U p to 1800 the only place of worship in the village of Leamington Priors and its population of 300 was the Parish Church of All Saints situated on the southern bank of the River Leam. For at least 500 years the then humble building had remained virtually unaltered - the earliest record of a vicar there is dated 1315. From 1800 onwards the Spa developed rapidly and the village was transformed. The arrival of large numbers of the rich, fashionable world, plus a huge increase in the working population necessitated a new order of things both in the social and in the religious sphere.

Apart from the obvious spiritual aspect, attendance at church or chapel was then also an essential part of social life. The rich were indeed religious-minded but they realized as well that it was important to attend church in order to see and be seen. Their servants however had no choice and were required to attend as a condition of their employment.

Linked with religious groups were the Band of Hope, Temperance and Self Improvement societies. Special services were held at the Public Hall, Windsor Street, on Sunday afternoons for carmen (drivers of horse vehicles), bathchairmen, grooms and stablemen and it seems that these meetings were extremely popular. The ministers, rather than fighting for social reform, sadly continued with the oppression of the poor. They preached obedience to their betters and contented acceptance of their wretched lot, though the chapels did at least provide a favourable focal point for the respectable poor.

Between 1800 and 1850 a large number of new churches and chapels appeared in the town namely five C.O.E. and eight Nonconformist. The C.O.E. had Christ Church, Upper Parade (1825), St. Mary's, off Radford Road (1839), Milverton Chapel ("Pepper Box" Chapel) Milverton Hill (1836), Holy Trinity, Beauchamp Avenue (1847), St. Luke's, Augusta Place (1850), while the Nonconformists had the Independent Chapel, Clemens Street 1816), Wesleyan Chapel, Portland Street (1826), Lady Huntingdon's Chapel, Mill Street (1829), Baptist Chapel, Guy Street (1830), Baptist Chapel, Warwick Street (1833), Congregational Chapel, Spencer Street (1836), Congregational Chapel,

Christ Church, Beauchamp Square, about 1910.

(continued page 66)

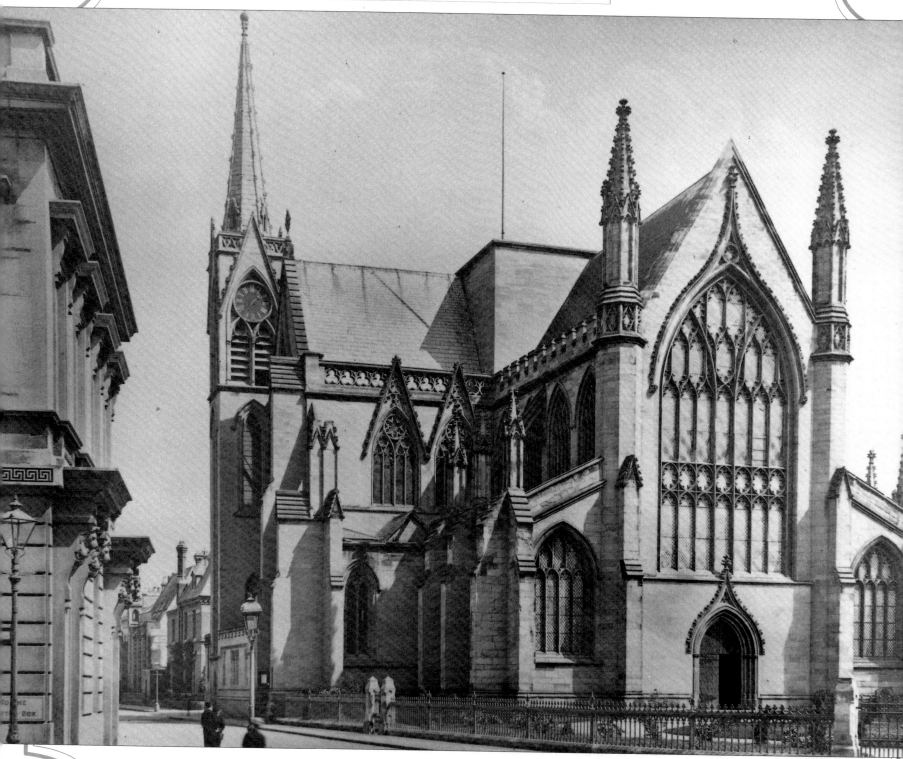

Parish Church, about 1890.

(above) Congregational Chapel, Spencer Street, about 1920.

(right) Wesleyan Chapel, Dale Street, interior, 1971.

Holly Walk (1849), and St. Peter's R.C. Chapel, George Street (1828).

The figures of the 1851 Census indicate a very healthy religious state in Leamington.

Salvation Army Citadel, Park Street, 1984.

There were then 7,604 seats available for about 48% of the population (15,700); approximately 75% of these were Anglican. A brief study of the impressive development of the Parish Church indicates the rapid increase in the size of the town and the resulting heavy demand for larger and more places of worship. The old church building was first extensively enlarged in 1816, followed by major improvements in 1826. However, by 1843 it was obvious that the existing structure could be enlarged no further and thus in that same year an entirely new and massive building was commenced, not being fully completed until 1869. Between 1898 and 1902 the church was made larger with the addition of two bays to the nave and a large western bell tower thus fulfilling Rev. John Craig's initial dream of erecting a building of cathedral-like proportions. Today it is one of the country's largest Parish churches.

In the early Victorian era it was frequently the practice to build churches at the central point of new development areas, thus creating an attractive and favourable feature that would encourage speculators to erect high-class houses in the area. Examples of such in Leamington were St. Mary's and Christ Church. During the period 1850-1900 the popularity of the Spa waned and the town then became more a place of permanent residence and continued to grow steadily in size so that by 1900 there was a population of about 26,000. Over the fifty years a great number of churches were built: Ebenezer Primitive Methodist, High Street (1852); Free Baptist Chapel, Clarendon Street (1863); United Methodist Free Church, Warwick Street (1863); St. Peter's (R.C.), Dormer Place (1864); Wesleyan Chapel, Dale Street (1870); St. Paul's, Leicester Street (1874); St. Alban's, Warwick Street (1877); St. John's,

St. Alban's Church, Warwick Street, about 1910.

Sunday School Demonstration, Jephson Garden's Pavilion, 1923.

Tachbrook Street (1877); Trinity Methodist, Radford Road (1877); St. Mark's, Rugby Road (1879); Salvation Army, Park Street (about 1880) and the Mission Chapel of the Good Shepherd, Satchwell Street (1890).

Sunday Schools associated with the various religious groups played an important part in the life and even the education of the children of the poor, especially during the first half of the 19th century.

GOING TO SCHOOL

At about 1800 there was virtually no education for the children of the "lower orders". Most families were desperately poor and parents did not encourage their children to attend for the very little schooling then available but rather sent them off to earn a little extra money by running errands, gleaning or collecting acorns for the pigs.

Initial thoughts about setting up schools for these children were not, in the main, prompted by a desire to help them but an urgent need to clear the town's fashionable streets of the dirty and unruly mobs of urchins.

The various religious groups and charities were the first in the field of education for the children of the poor. If they wished they could at least receive basic instruction in reading and possibly writing once a week at Sunday School and, later on, the earliest day schools were run mainly by the local churches and chapels. The earliest schools were: All Saints C.O.E. (1822), the only Day School until 1838 (attendance was voluntary and fees were between two and four pence according to age), two nondenominational Infant Schools, in Guy Street and

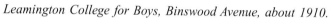

Leamington College for Boys, Binswood Avenue, about 1910.

The School Room

The Gymnasium

Collegiate School for Boys, Warwick Street, 1890.

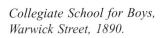

The Laboratory

The Dining Room

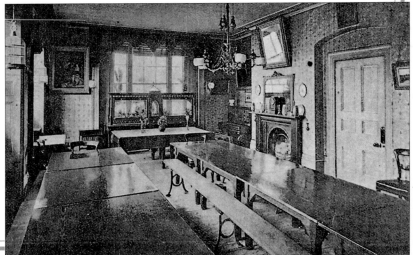

Wesleyan School, Portland Street, 1910.

Ranelagh Terrace (1834). The Wesleyans set up the town's second Day School (Windsor Street, 1838) and then, between 1840 and 1870, a further twelve Church Day Schools were established.

Hopper, in his guide of 1842, makes much of the amount of free education given to the children of Leamington: "There is a commendable solicitude in regard to the education of youth". When education for the poor was very much in its infancy he was possibly right to be proud that 1800 children from a town population of 13,000 (one sixth) were receiving education. Actually, only about 800 youngsters attended a day school, the remaining 1000 had to make do with instruction at Sunday School.

The schools for the rich and poor were all of a very low academic standard and teachers were usually poorly qualified.

By the 1860's life for working-class children had improved; more and more were able to attend school as their parents became less dependant on the income gained by the work of their offspring.

Board School, Rugby Road, about 1915.

During the 19th century the town had an abundance of private schools of varying size and character. Twenty eight were listed in 1851 while in 1883 there were no less than 45. The most important of these were the Boys' College, Binswood Avenue (1847) and the then small Arnold Lodge Preparatory School, Kenilworth Road (1864).

In the private schools cruelty and bullying was rife and were places of dread for the unfortunate pupils. Some children were luckier as they received instruction in more pleasant conditions at home from a tutor or governess, while very young ones were soon put out of the way in kindergarten schools run by Dames who were, in effect, nothing but childminders.

General education was rapidly introduced during the period 1870-1900, the impetus provided by the 1870 Elementary Education Act when the government sought to establish a school within easy reach of every child in the country. They were to be under the control of a local Board and be nondenominational.

In 1880, after many schools had been built, attendance was made compulsory although many poorer children still stayed away to do full-time jobs, begging or pilfering. Fees for elementary education were abolished in 1891. In the thirty years following 1870 four large Board Schools were established: Clapham Terrace (capacity 1000), Leicester Street (1050), Shrubland Street (1080) and Rugby Road (510). Four new Church Schools were also formed. William Street (Congregational), Court Street (Wesleyan), St. Johns, Tachbrook Street (C.O.E.) and St. Mary's Girls and Infants, New Street (C.O.E.). Around 1900 Leamington had four colleges, these being the Boys' College, Binswood Avenue, the High School for Girls (later Kingsley), 19 the Parade, the Collegiate School, Warwick Street and Greyfriars School, Beech Lawn, Warwick Street.

MEMORABLE OCCASIONS

In the first half of the 19th century most of the ordinary folk of Leamington spent their entire lives in and around the town. There was little opportunity to travel and therefore their interests and activities were very much a local affair while external events of a national or worldwide nature generally tended to be remote. Long before the advent of radio, television and the telephone the only media was the newspaper but even that was too costly for the working man.

Any local event, even if mediocre by modern standards, had a tremendous appeal and were highlights in an otherwise dreary existence.

Civic occasions with their pomp and colour excited both rich and poor alike. The whole town turned out to line the streets to greet visiting Royalty with tumultuous cheers e.g. the visit of the Prince Regent, later George IV, in 1819, and that of Princess Victoria, aged 11, in

Laying of foundation stone of Parish Church extension, 1898.

1830 and again in 1858 when she was Queen. There were also impressive celebrations to commemorate the happy day on May 24th 1837 when the Princess Victoria attained, at the age of 18, her legal majority. A public holiday was declared, bells rang out everywhere and thousands joined in the day's events. A mile-long procession marched through the streets which were decorated with flags and banners and colourful flowers graced all the balconies. 2,050 of the working classes sat down to an open air dinner in the Newbold Pleasure Grounds (later Jephsons) and a tea party for 2,200 children followed in the afternoon. A further and even more splendid day was June 28th, 1838 when Queen Victoria's coronation was celebrated.

May 29th, 1856 was a memorable day when imposing arrangements were made to mark the end of the Crimean War. These included a public procession through the town (every child receiving the gift of a straw hat or a bonnet), a cooked dinner and a childrens' tea party in the Jephson Gardens for working class families, decoration of the streets, music in the day and a fireworks display in the evening.

In July 1838 a deputation arrived back in Leamington from London after receiving from Queen Victoria the gracious concession which entitled the town to use the "Royal" prefix. In

Coronation Day (K.G.V.), 1911.

High Street a large crowd, brimming with joy and excitement received the news with loud cheers; the horses were removed from the carriage carrying the two-man deputation and it was then pulled by the rejoicing crowd to the Regent Hotel where several thousand people awaited to hear the address, "the cheering rolling along the streets like volleys of thunder".

The great engineer Isambard Kingdom Brunel was host at a celebration dinner at the Regent Hotel in 1852 to mark the inauguration of the G.W.R. line which linked Leamington to London and Birmingham.

The official opening of the Jephson Gardens in 1846 was a day when "the weather was glorious, the bells were ringing without pause, the Parades, from one end to the other, were thronged with holiday folk. Leamington

National Union of Railwaymen procession, Warwick Street, 1914.

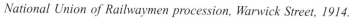

was once more in one of its exuberant moods!" A procession more than half a mile long left the High Street Town Hall and paraded the town, finally arriving at the Gardens where about 7,000 were gathered. Another grand function took place in the Gardens in 1849 when the statue of Dr. H. Jephson was unveiled. It was a fine day and crowds of people attended the archery fête, horticultural show, cricket matches and musical entertainment. Similar excitement occurred in 1853 when the foundation stone of the Windsor Street Public Hall was laid when "the day was observed as a holiday, the bells of the Parish Church were rung merrily and the decorations of the town imparted a joyous and festive appearance to the principal streets". On a Sunday morning in 1847 Holy Trinity Church, Beauchamp Avenue was officially opened and in the evening about 70 people were entertained at the Town Hall, High Street; most of these being workmen who had built the church.

Whenever there was a national Royal occasion it followed that the town being "Royal", should seize the opportunity to stage a grand show and express its loyalty with special joy and fervour. Such events were the marriage of the Prince of Wales (later Ed. VII) and Princess Alexandra, 1863; the marriage of the Duke of York (later Geo. V) and Princess Mary of Teck, 1893; the Diamond jubilee of Queen Victoria, 1897; the Coronation of King Edward VII, 1902; and that of King George V, 1911. Empire Day was always an important annual event - especially for the children.

Funeral of T.T. Earnshaw, Chief Constable, Bath Street, 1938.

Sir Winston Churchill in Leamington, 1945.

Various other local happenings were well supported, such as workers' and church rallies, processions, carnivals, gymkhanas and flower shows. There were also great festivities when the new Town Hall on the Parade was opened in 1884.

Special occasions of a family nature were, of course, of much interest to the people concerned. In the main these events were weddings, christenings and funerals but summer outings were also important. Photographs of the happy days were often taken with everyone appearing very camera-conscious and uncomfortable in their unaccustomed finery.

(continued page79)

V.E. Day Street Party in , Norfolk Street 1945. Included in photograph are Mrs Abbot, Jill Bartlet, Ron Boalch, Mrs Bosworth, Bill Bosworth, Dorothy Clarke, Fred Clarke, Janice Clarke, Joy Clarke, Val Clarke, Mrs Goddard, Mrs Hartwell, Baby Pam Hartwell, Barry Hartwell, Marjorie Hughes, June Hughes, Mrs Lloyd, Dora Lloyd, Mrs Tarver, Mrs Frank West, Mrs West (Hill Street).

SIGNS OF THE PAST

INTRODUCTION

Not everyone is inclined to browse through ponderous books on local history but they can at least trace something of past events and people by examining the various commemorative inscriptions displayed in public places around Leamington. The town is quite fortunate in having a large number of these, many of which record people who, in more ways than one, have left their mark. Such well-known figures as Satchwell, Jephson, Willes, Flavel and Eden together with Royal names like Victoria, Mary, Adelaide, York, Prince of Wales and Earl Spencer all appear to tell their own story. On a sombre note there are, for example, the various War Memorials which honour those who gave their lives for their country and for freedom. Almost all of Leamington's inscriptions are listed but no doubt a number of others have been missed in the survey.

Neatly-dressed local lads rest awhile on New River Walk beside the lazy River Leam. Behind the trees a partial view of the grand Victorian villas of Warwick New Road. The year is about 1895.

BRIDGES

Victoria Bridge. Stone tablet on parapet, South East side, according to T.B. Dudley (1896) the inscription read: "This stone was laid by Henry Jephson, M.D. on the 25th May, 1840 in commemoration of the extension of this bridge and in celebration of the Birthday of Her Most Gracious Majesty, Queen Victoria" [the Queen's actual birthday was the 24th May].

Today the inscription is "... and in celebration of the visit of..." Perhaps a new stone, with modified wording has been inserted since Dudley's Book of 1896? One contemporary writer says that the stone disappeared during the night following the stone-laying! "It had not been removed at 3 o'clock at which hour some of the night watch were near to the spot". A frantic search was initiated and it was revealed eventually that the missing tablet had not been stolen but merely "removed". It was returned safely the following day and duly reinstated in its original position. One tale says that the stone had been thrown into the river.

Victoria Bridge, about 1910.

The Mill Weir and Suspension Bridge, about 1950.

Mill Suspension Bridge (footbridge) and adjoining Mill Gardens. Stone tablet on the South West end of the bridge: "Opened June 1903 by Alderman Davis (Mayor, W.G.) Wm. DeNormanville, Engineer."

York Bridge (footbridge). Stone tablet on the North West end: "This bridge and Promenade were opened by Alderman J. Hinks, J.P., Mayor, July 6th 1893. W. DeNormanville, Engineer."

Willes Road Bridge. Stone tablet in the centre of the West parapet: "This tablet was placed here by the inhabitants of Leamington, to record the munificence of

York Bridge and Pump Room Gardens during 1932 floods. The river rose 20 feet.

Edward Willes Esquire, of Newbold Comyn, to whom the town is indebted for the site of the adjoining public Gardens (Jephsons - W.G.), for this bridge and road and many other valuable gifts". [No date specified but bridge was built 1827, improved 1876-W.G.].

Princes Drive Bridge. Bronze plaque on the parapet of the South West side: (plaque had disappeared-stolen?-by 1982). (Above text: Borough Coat of Arms) "Borough of Royal Leamington Spa Prince's Bridge. This bridge was opened for traffic on June 14th, 1923 by the Mayor (Councillor G.W. Hawkins-W.G.). The Trussed Concrete Steel Co. Ltd., Structural Engineers. A. Jackaman and Sons Ltd., Slough, Contractors. Ald. W. Davis, J.P., Chairman of the Highway Committee. J.J. Kennan, C.E., Borough Engineer."

Note: a smaller bronze plaque is believed to have been attached to the parapet on the North West side but, at about 1980, there were only filled-in screw holes (plaque stolen earlier?). It is assumed that this plaque mentioned the Royal

Adelaide Bridge and York Promenade, about 1910.

opening of the Bridge by H.R.H. the Prince of Wales (later Edward VIII) sometime in 1923.

Water Works, Campion Terrace – large stone figures over main door: ("1878") with the Borough Coat of Arms between 18 and 78.

Adelaide Bridge. Stone on the parapet of the North West side: "This bridge, having been rebuilt, was opened by the Mayor J. Hinks, J.P., August 13th 1891. W. DeNormanville, Engineer."

Willes Bridge, about 1900.

BUILDINGS

Art Gallery and Museum. Large plaque in vestibule: "This Art Gallery erected from funds provided by voluntary subscription and the Rates in equal proportions, was opened 6th December 1928 by Sir Charles Holmes, K.C.B., Director of the National Gallery, Alfred Holt M.A., J.P., C.C., Mayor, J.H.W. Southey, Lt. Col., O.B.E., Chairman, A.C. Bunch, F.R.I.B.A., Architect, W.E. Owen, Curator."

Bath Assembly Hall. Stones high up on facade: "The Bath Assembly Hall built 1926".

Binswood Hall, ex-Boys' College, Binswood Avenue. On the wall in the Assembly Hall, a tablet: "To commemorate the achievements of Sir Frank Whittle, K.B.E., C.B., F.R.S., who by his inventions placed his country in the forefront of aeronautics. A pupil of this school 1918-1923." Frank Whittle is world-famous for his pioneer work on jet engines for aircraft.

British Legion (Royal), Irwin Hall, Kenilworth Street. Plaque over front entrance: "In memory of Ronald J.B. Irwin, D.S.O., M.C., Chaplain and Assistant Chaplain General to the Forces in the Great War and Chairman of the Warwickshire Council of the British Legion 1925-27".

Clarendon Square, No 6. Blue and white round plaque mounted on house facade in 1985: "Warwick District Council, Charles Louis Napoleon Bonaparte (1808-1873), Napoleon III, Emperor of the French, stayed here 1838-1839."

Conservative Club, 36 Warwick Street.

Bath Assembly Rooms, Spencer Street, 1956.

Decorative plaque on the North wall. Plaque has large centre piece which features the head of the Greek Goddess Athene (Minerva of the Romans) with her name above it 'AqHNA' . The history of this plaque is obscure but it is believed the building was at one time a library.

Denby Buildings, Regent Grove. A feature in the stonework over central archway: "Denby Buildings" and on building to the West of the pinnacled tower, east-end of block, high up: stone tablet "1885".

Adelaide Bridge. Opening of rebuilt bridge by Mayor Coun. J. Hinks, J.P., 13th August 1891. Note in foreground man on horseback and boy with penny farthing bicycle.

County Fire Brigade Headquarters, Warwick Street: a carved hardwood panel in vestibule:" County Fire Brigade Headquarters-opened by Sir John Hobson, O.B.E., T.D., Q.C., M.P., on the 18th July, 1962".

Jephson Housing Association H.Q., Dormer Place. Tablet on the South West corner of the building facing the Pump Room Gardens: "5-7 Dormer Place, completed 3rd June, 1977. This building occupies the site of two former town houses built circa 1840 and destroyed by a single, high explosive bomb dropped by an enemy aircraft on the evening of 14th November, 1940". This was during the night of the Coventry Blitz.

Lansdowne Crescent: large metal plaque on a post erected 1981 in the front garden area: "William Thomas 1799-1860. One of Canada's most prominent architects, Thomas was born in Suffolk and apprenticed as a carpenter before establishing an extensive architectural practice here in Royal Leamington Spa. During the 1830's he designed a series of attractive residences including this grand neoclassical crescent, Lansdowne Circus, Comyn Lodge, Aberdeen House and the Masonic Rooms. In 1843, frustrated by a depression in the building industry, Thomas emigrated to Toronto, Canada. He soon gained widespread recognition as the architect of many outstanding public and ecclesiastical buildings as well as numerous commercial and residential structures. Unrivalled in his mastery of detail, Thomas became the leading exponent in the country of the Decorated Gothic Revival style and designed some of the finest buildings erected in Ontario during the nineteenth century. Erected by the Ontario Heritage Foundation, Ministry of Culture and Recreation, Ontario, Canada."

Public Library, Avenue Road. Stone tablet on left side of main entrance: "Opened December 12th 1902 by Sir Oliver Lodge, D.Sc., F.R.S., Principal of the University of Birmingham. Alderman William Davis, C.C. Mayor. Alderman T.W. Thursfield, M.D., J.P. Chairman of the Library Committee, Councillor J.T. Barrett, Chairman of the Technical Committee". Tablet to right of main entrance: "This stone was laid by Alderman James Murray Molesworth, Mayor of Leamington October 30th 1900. J. Mitchell Bottomley, Architect, R. Bowen, Builder."

Parade. Present No 118 (Dunns). Blue and white round plaque mounted on facade in 1985:- "Warwick District Council. Dr. Henry Jephson (1798-1878) Physician and Philanthropist lived here 1825-1839".

Parish Church (All Saints). Two foundation stones, side by side, on the West end of the nave: "To the Glory of God and in the faith of Jesus Christ this stone of the two western bays and the western tower of this church was duly laid on Thursday June 30th 1898 – by the Mayor of Leamington Gordon Lyon Bland in memory of the long and prosperous reign of Victoria Queen of England and Empress of India LAUS DEO".

(left) Parish Church from Gloucester Street, around 1890. Shows church as completed 1869.

Also in the western forecourt of the church is a flowering tree with a small plaque in the ground:- "This tree was planted by the All Saints' Guide Company to commemorate the Coronation 1953" [Queen Elizabeth II].

Above the south porch a stone shield which, according to Notcutt's Guide 1923 has inscribed "an ingenious combination of letters standing for "John Craig, Vicar". An identical shield was, until about 1970, situated above the porch of the Gospel Hall, Priory Terrace - a reminder of the building's original function as the Vicar's Grammar School (1848). The cathedral-like Parish Church was the brainchild of the Rev. Craig.

In the graveyard, just South of church: (a) Tomb – "This sacred tribute of a daughter's love and duty is raised to the memory of Benjamin Satchwell, of Leamington Priors; who departed this life December 1, 1810 in the seventy seventh year of his age".

An earlier tomb, surrounded by iron railings, carried the same inscription except that 1815 then appeared instead of 1810; also, on the opposite side was an elegy by R.J. Pratt. J.C. Manning in his book "Glimpses of our Local Past," 1895, points out a curious error on this tomb and suggests a probable explanation. He established that Ben actually died in 1810 yet the tomb, as in 1895, gave 1815 as the year of death. Manning then mentions R.J. Pratt's Guide (1812) in which it is stated that Ben died in 1815 and that the tomb was already in existence. It seemed strange to him that a book published in 1812 should record an event that oc-

Church Walk and Parish Church. The two houses, (behind Aylesford Well) demolished about 1890. On the right the Courier Office.

curred in the future (1815)! His solution to the mystery was that the date 1815 was simply a printers' error and because the Guide book was used as a reference when the tomb was inscribed, the original mistake was perpetuated. After the lapse of about 80 years the record was at last righted as a new tomb was erected, presumably in 1902, to replace the ancient original described by Manning in 1895. The wording of the new main inscription was as before except that the correct year of 1810 was stated. The elegy however was not reinstated but was replaced with the following: "Benjamin Satchwell, who among many other charitable acts founded in the year 1806 the Leamington Spa Charity which excellent Institution developed into the present Warneford Hospital A.D. 1902" [presumably this is the date of the new tomb].

Yet a further modification to the tomb was carried out later. The west end was inscribed thus: "The tomb was renovated to mark the 150th Anniversary of the death of Benjamin Satchwell 1st December 1960".

(b) William Abbotts is also buried nearby but his tomb stone has not survived. The tomb inscription read "Behold the tomb of William Abbotts! Who died the first of March, 1805, aged sixty-nine: first founder of the celebrated Spa Water Baths at this place in 1786. He devoted his whole time and fortune to accommodate the public, and lived to see his benevolent works merit the approbation of the most eminent physicians."

Abbotts' New Inn, later Bath Hotel, 1825.

On the church wall, west of the south porch, is a granite tablet: "Near this stone are interred the remains of John Frederick Perkins Flavel died 2nd March 1831, aged 19 and of William Henry Flavel, died 23rd June 1832 aged 24. Sons of William Flavel of this town (Inventor of the Kitchener) and of Edith Frances his wife. R.I.P." The Kitchener referred to was the famous Patent Kitchener which earned for William Flavel many Prize Medals. An 1830 catalogue describes the cast iron

The Parade with Regent Hotel, about 1920.

cooking range as "a register cooking-grate constructed on new and improved principles by W. Flavel, Ironmonger and Commission Agent, Bath Street, Leamington, and adapted to all fire-places, from three to ten feet in length."

Police Headquarters, Hamilton Terrace. A framed certificate in vestibule "Warwick-shire Police Authority, Divisional Police Headquarters, Leamington Spa. I declare this Police Headquarters to be open (signed) E.I. England, Mayor of the Borough of Royal Leamington Spa. Alderman Miss E.I. England, O.B.E. Dated this second day of October, 1968." Also on certificate the coat of Arms of Warwickshire and of the Borough of Royal Leamington Spa.

Regent Hotel, Parade. In the foyer two large panels can be found carrying many names of famous people who were guests at Hotel. "Our heritage is our Visitors. This panel was unveiled by Earl Spencer, M.V.O.D.L., 17th November, 1984."

Railway Station (B.R. previously G.W.R.). In booking hall there is a clock – repositioned about 1975 - and under clock is a metal plaque:- "This clock was presented to the Great Western Railway by the Corporation of Royal Leamington Spa to commemorate the completion of the new station buildings - 1939".

Great Western Railway Station. Demolition and rebuilding 1936-38.

Salvation Army Citadel, Park Street (Erected c.1881 - Demolished 1984). Inside the building, in the rear portion and on the south wall a tablet: "To the memory of Miss Sarah Harvey died Feb. 1, 1880, by whose generosity this building has been provided for the Salvation Army and the people of Leamington. To God be the Glory."

Swimming Bath, Pump Room. Stone tablet on east end of bath. This was removed c.1960 but it is believed to have read "Opened by J. Fell, Mayor 1890." (J. Fell was, for a second time, Mayor 1889-1890).

Swimming Bath opened by Mayor John Fell, 1890.

In the ground floor vending area there is, on the wall a tablet:-"This plaque was unveiled on 27th October, 1956 by the Prime Minister the R. Hon. Anthony Eden, K.G., M.C., MP., to commemorate the reconstruction of the Swimming Bath, originally opened in 1890 by John Fell, Mayor. L.G. Clayton, Chairman Spa Committee; E.A. Baxter, Mayor".

Earl of Avon arriving to open Royal Spa Centre, 15th. June 1972.

At each of the four corners are the Heraldic bearings of the de Clinton, Dudley, Fisher and Willes families. All these had in historic times been Lords of the Manor of Leamington and their bearings were incorporated in the design of the Borough Arms in 1876.

Royal Spa Centre. Newbold Terrace. Two marble tablets inside:

(a) In basement: "This stone was laid by Hugh Willott, M.A., Secretary General of the Arts Council of Great Britain on 16th November 1970".

(b)   In foyer: "This building was opened on 15th June 1972 by The Right Hon. The Earl of Avon, K.G., P.C., M.C." (Anthony Eden, one time MP. for Warwick & Leamington, also Prime Minister).

St. Lukes Congregational Church, Hamilton Terrace (now converted to offices):

(a)   Beside the west doorway: "The erection of this Congregational Church was commenced March 23rd 1849. The Revd. Henry Batchelor Pastor.

(b)   Beside the east doorway: "This stone was laid by the Revd. Henry Batchelor on the 3rd April, MDCCCXLIX.

St. Pauls Church, Leicester Street. Stone at the north-east corner of the church: "To the Glory of God. This foundation stone of St. Paul's Church was laid by William Willes Esq., 15th May, 1873." A tablet on a building to the west of the church "St. Pauls Parochial Rooms and Church House" (In the 1920's the building was used as St. Paul's Infant School).

Town Hall, Parade. Foundation stone under front portico on the South side: "This stone was laid by Alderman Henry Bright, J.P., Mayor of Leamington, Oct. 17th 1882". Inside the Town Hall, in the vestibule a tablet: "Randolph Adolphus Turpin, Born 7th June, 1928, Died 17th May 1966. World Middleweight Boxing Champion 1951. A resident of this town. Presented by D.J. Bradshaw, Esq., 10th July, 1979".

Urquhart Hall, corner of Leam Terrace and Mill Street. Tablet on north wall, Leam Terrace side "CHRISTUS VERUM FUNDAMENTUM SIT HUIC DOMO FIRMAMENTUM". This stone was laid in the faith of Jesus Christ and the hope of his blessing on this building by Mary Urquhart, daughter of the donor Sarah Urquhart, Ascension Eve 1905."

Randolph A. Turpin on the Town Hall porch after becoming World Middleweight Champion, 1951. Mayor Ald. O.R. Davidson on the right.

(above) Urquhart Hall, Leam Terrace, about 1970.

(below) The Parthenon (Lower Assembly Rooms 1821), Bath Street. In rebuilt state after 1969 fire.

JEPHSON GARDENS

Main gates at Lower Parade. There are 2 bronze shield plaques on the gates: (a) North side of gates a small Borough Coat of Arms then "These gates were presented by Rowland Sydney Salt, Chairman, Parks and Gardens Committee 1948". (b) South side of gates on the front of a shield: large Borough Coat of Arms, on rear of this shield, "Borough of Royal Leamington Spa, Jephson Gardens opened 1846."

In the Gardens there are the following features:- Statue of Henry Jephson, M.D., by Hollins, inside Corinthian Temple (1849) on the plinth of the statue: "Henry Jephson, M.D., 1798-1878". (The date of death, 1878, was added).

Clock Tower with Westminster chimes at the west-end of main lawn. Tablet on the South side "Presented by Mrs. William Davis, to the memory of her late husband, William Davis, J.P. 15 years Councillor and 28 years Alderman, three times Mayor and 27 years Chairman of the Highways Committee of this Borough, 1925".

Floral Clock situated to the South of the main pathway, South of the Jephson Temple. Plaque set in

Entrance lodges and gates about 1910. Willes Obelisk in the distance.

Willes Obelisk with Pump Rooms and Hitchman Fountain, about 1910.

ground: "Dedicated to those who have loved and tended these Gardens and in Memory of SARAH M. PURCELL, Mayoress of this Borough 1947-1949. This floral clock was installed in the Festival of Britain Year 1951".

Czech Memorial to the West of Jephson Temple. A large bronze plaque on a block of rough granite, facing onto a water fountain, the top part of which is shaped as a parachute and the stream of water from the top falls down

Hitchman Fountain with Newbold
Terrace behind, about 1890.

Jephson Temple.

grooves, then in open air to represent the cords of a parachute. On this stone 'parachute' are inscribed the names of members of the mission-as described in the wording of the plaque:- "In tribute to all the Czechoslovak soldiers, airmen and patriots who fell in World War II. From Leamington Spa, in 1941, volunteers from Free Czechoslovak Forces stationed in the town, were parachuted into their homeland to rid it of the tyrant "Protector" S.S. General Heydrich. Two of them JAN KUBIŠ and JOSEF GABČÍK - accomplished their mission in May, 1942. They and their companions laid down their lives FOR FREEDOM." Plans for the assassination of Heydrich were made in a house in Newbold Terrace. Near this monument is a rosebed which has two plaques (a) Bronze plaque "Lidice shall live. Garden of Remembrance. 25th anniversary 1967". The furious Nazis totally destroyed the village of Lidice as retribution for

the killing of Heydrich. (b) A stone tablet: "1940-45 Great Britain-Luxembourg, in remembrance and as a mark of friendship to the town of Royal Leamington Spa. League of Luxembourg Volunteers of War in Great Britain."

Arbour – on the North side of the main lawn, near Newbold Terrace gates: "1969 – This Arbour was donated to the town by Mrs. H.M. Gee in memory of her husband Frank Gee who died on May 9th 1965".

Statue of Dr. Henry Jephson, about 1952.

Hitchman Fountain. Situated in the North West corner of the Gardens, near Lower Parade. Inscribed around large central marble column: "In memory of Doctor John Hitchman who died March 1867" (there is no sign of the name of the architect, John Cundall, or of its sculptor. Fountain unveiled 1869).

Willes Obelisk. Situated along the main walk, near to the lake. West side: "Erected in honour of Edward Willes, Esq., of Newbold Comyn, to whom Leamington is indebted for the site of these Gardens". North side "1875". Both inscriptions are repeated on opposite sides.

In the gardens there are also quite a few small plaques associated with a tree or flower bed – planted in memory of a local person or some other commemoration. The following are some of them, there are many others:- The R.A.F. rose bed, the Life Boat rose bed (150th Anniversary of the Royal National Life Boat Institution), Flowering Cherry: "A loyal tribute to Queen Elizabeth II in her Coronation Year 1953". Tree commemorating H.M. Queen Elizabeth, the Queen Mother, 80th Birthday 4th August 1980. Silver Birch, rear of Jephson Temple: "This silver birch was planted by His Worship the Mayor of Royal Leamington Spa, Councillor George Purcell. To mark the occasion of the marriage of H.R.H the Princess Elizabeth K.G., and H.R.H. the Duke of Edinburgh K.G., November 20th 1947. Strength and beauty met together". Maple Tree: "Dedicated to the memory of PTE. HENRY TANDY, V.C., D.C.M., M.M. 1892-1977". Tulip Tree: "Presented by the Leamington Society as a tribute to George Ingle who as Parks Director to the Borough of Royal Leamington Spa cherished these Gardens 1945-1968". Maple Tree. 'This tree was planted on the 5th June 1971 by Jack Jones, General Secretary of the Transport and General Workers Union, in commemoration of the Conference held in Leamington Spa in 1921 at which a number of Unions amalgamated to form the Transport and General Workers Union".

(right) Davis memorial Clock Tower, about 1930.
(below) The Czech memorial. The Mayor Alderman Miss E. I. England O.B.E., at the unveiling 26th October 1968.

MEMORIALS

Lord Aylesford's Well (Camden's Well) site of the old Well House with "The original spring recorded by Camden 1586" above entrance, was demolished in 1960 and in its place was erected in 1963 a small stone pillar having "This stone commemorates the Aylesford Well (also known as Camdens Well) erected in 1813 (1803? W.G.) by the fifth Earl of Aylesford. The building was demolished in 1960. The first record of the spring of curative natural saline water which was on this site was made by Camden in 1586. Presented by the National

(left) Aylesford Well, with early Courier Office in Church Walk, on right, about 1910.

(below) Inscribed stone at present on site of Aylesford Spring, 1984.

(top) *Spa Water Drinking Fountain, next to Pump Room, 1984.*
(above) *Tablet on the Bright Obelisk, 1984.*
(right) *Henry Bright, Mayor, admires his Obelisk, 1880.*

Town Hall and Bright Obelisk, about 1900.

Association of Master Monumental Masons in Conference at Royal Leamington Spa, September 1963". Under the text is an illustration of the old Well House.

Bright Obelisk, Parade. On the marble base is: (a) front - above drinking fountain, now sealed off - "Erected by public subscription to record the services of Alderman Henry Bright to whose untiring exertions this town is chiefly indebted for its supply of pure water". (b) rear:- "1880".

Lawn Tennis.

(a) Tablet on a stone pillar on the Manor House Hotel lawn, opposite to hotel main entrance, "In 1872 Major Harry Gem and his friend Mr. J.B. Pereira joined with Dr. Frederick Haynes and Dr. A. Wellesley Tomkins to found the first lawn tennis club in the world and played the game on nearby lawns. This plaque was erected on the occasion of the centenary celebrations on the 11th June 1972".

(b) Bronze tablet on low wall separating grounds of Manor House Hotel and those of Manor Court Flats. This is a copy of the original [erected 1930's] which it is assumed was taken by a souvenir hunter some years previous. The copy was unveiled in August 1963 and a duplicate passed to the Town Hall for safe keeping. The inscription reads "The Manor House Hotel. On this lawn the first Lawn Tennis Club in the world was founded in 1872".

(c) Hamilton Terrace. On a small plot of land (east of the Police Station) which is the site of Major H. Gem's house, Arran Villa, 5 Hamilton Terrace - the tablet is mounted on a stone pillar facing roadway: "Major Harry Gem lived in a house on this site from 1872 until his death in 1881. In 1872 he founded in Leamington the first Lawn Tennis Club in the world and was its first president. This plaque was erected on the occasion of the centenary celebrations of 11th June 1972."

ROYAL PUMP ROOM
AND BATHS

(above) Aerial photograph about 1930 showing the Manor House Lawns where the world's first Lawn Tennis Club played in 1872. Site now occupied by Manor Court.

(right) August 26, 1963, unveiling of plaque in the grounds of Manor House Hotel to commemorate the founding there of the world's first Lawn Tennis Club, 1872.

(left) This sketch was made by Harry Gem, the President and founder of the Leamington Club, the first lawn tennis club in the world. The picture shows Harry Gem himself, on the left near the net, with his friend Jean-Baptiste Pereira playing against Dr. Wellesley Tomkins, near the net, and Dr. Frederick Haynes both of Warneford Hospital. This was the first game played when the club was inaugurated in the summer of 1872 on the lawns of the Manor House Hotel.

Queen Victoria statue, Parade. Inscription on a granite plinth: Front: "Victoria Queen Empress 1837-1901 She wrought her people lasting good". Rear: "Erected by the people of Leamington October 11th 1902 William Davis, Mayor".

The sculptor's name appears at the base of actual statue: "Albert Toft 1902" (Statue unveiled by Lord Leigh 1902). On the north side of plinth is a small metal plaque: "A German bomb moved this statue one inch on its plinth on the 14th November 1940" (night of Coventry Blitz). Statue cleaned 1984.

Spa Water Fountain, south of Pump Room. There is a small stone pillar, about 4ft high, sited on the pavement between the Pump Room and the River Leam. There is a tap for the supply of Spa Water. Inscription on pillar reads "Spa Drinking Water - 1964".

Victoria Park. Inside the Park near to the two entrances from Avenue Road and Archery Road are two large boulders. On each of these is a bronze plaque: "(Borough coat of arms), Borough of Royal Leamington Spa. This Avenue of trees was planted in memory of those men and women of Leamington Spa who fell in the World War 1939-1945". [I understand that these 2 boulders were found in a sand pit at Lillington and that they are volcanic rock; carried from Norway during one of the Ice Ages].

War Memorial, Euston Place. "To our fallen heroes 1914-1918, 1939-45, Korean War 1950-1953, Falklands Campaign 1982. Listed are the names of all those who died".

Warwickshire Royal Horse Artillery. On the playing field, corner of Lillington Road, a bronze plaque on a rough block of granite about 3ft high, "Warwickshire Royal Horse Artillery, T.F.,

War memorial, Euston Place, on the day of its unveiling 27th. May 1922.

Trade mark of the British Electric Traction Co., on a column in Avenue Road 1953. The column once supported the power lines of the Electric Tramway.

Hamilton Terrace, about 1900, showing Willes monument on right and the Crimean cannon.

Mayor Coun. Val Davis, Fred Hawkins and Dickie Friend view at the Town Hall the newly-erected plaque presented to Leamington in Remembrance and as a mark of friendship, by the League of Luxembourg Volunteers of War in Great Britain. November 1985.

FLANDERS 1914 COLOGNE 1918. (With badge of the Horse Artillery) - To all who served, lest we forget. Unveiled by R. Hon. Earl of Avon K.G. M.C. 1967".

Willes Monument. Hamilton Terrace, on the grass opposite present Police Station. Monument demolished about 1950. White's Directory for Warwickshire 1874, P.713, 714: states "Opposite to Hamilton Terrace ..., on an open grass plot, surrounded by a cluster of trees, stands a stone pillar, enclosed within iron palisades and surmounted by a gas lamp. The pillar bears the following inscription: "These trees were preserved by Edward Willes, Esq., of Newbold Comyn at the request of John and Sarah Williams, who by their spirit and industry, character and conduct, raised and established the Regent Hotel".

Private H. "Napper" Tandy VC,DCM,MM (far left), reputed most decorated British Army Private. He is standing with Coun. E.M. Kerry, Chairman Warwick District Council and Coun. Tom Williams, Mayor when the Royal Regiment of Fusiliers exercised its deed of privilege handed on by the Royal Warwickshire Regiment by marching through Leamington with drums beating, bayonets fixed and colours flying, 1st July 1976. The occasion coincided with the 60th anniversary of the battle of the Somme.

ON THE MOVE

INTRODUCTION

The great advances made over the years in various means of transport have each had a powerful effect upon the progress of Leamington. The stage coach, the canal, railways and motor cars have each in their time contributed to the speedy and economical conveyance of passengers and goods. Without doubt these developments have been one of the major factors in the growth and changing lifestyle of the town.

In recent years there has been a tremendous increase nationally in the number of transport preservation enthusiasts and, thanks to their dedicated efforts, both young and old are now able to relive the brave early days of invention and enterprise.

Neatly dressed children find welcome shelter from the sun's heat in the graceful avenue of Holly Walk. On the right is Brandon Parade and in the distance is the junction with Willes Road. The year is about 1890.

BY FOOT AND BY HORSE

During the centuries prior to 1800 few changes had affected the sleepy village of Leamington Priors. Transport was of little importance and was of a local nature. The appalling state of the approach roads kept Leamington in a position of almost total isolation and not a single stage coach passed within two miles of the place. A single smithy and a wheelwright's shop were adequate for the small number of agricultural carts and waggons. The farmers rode on horseback while the rustics used Shank's Pony.

Light loads were carried in by packhorse. With the growth of the new Spa in the early 1800's the roads entering Leamington were dramatically improved and consequently the old tranquil atmosphere departed forever.

Local entrepreneur and poet James Bisset, having a lively wit, produced numerous comic poems on town life. He applied his poetic treatment to the subject of transport and the result appears in the Guide published by him in 1816. It would seem from the following lines, that the arrangements were quite primitive; those engaged in the business were Messrs. Brown, Grant and Benton:-

Traffic problems in the Lower Parade, 1846.

Accommodation for Old and Young
For those who're lame, or have the gout,
Or those who cannot walk about,
Here's Brown and Grant, and either man
Will help you to a neat sedan.
There are donkeys, too, to let for hire,
At any hour you may require;
As also Gigs, or Donkey-chaise,
To drive out where, or when you please.
But what for Belles or Macaronies,
So fit as Benton's pretty Ponies?

Smart's Marble Baths, Clemens Street, about 1817.
Showing sedan chair, chariot and a carriage.

Lower Union Parade 1850.

The first London-Leamington stage coach, the "Eclipse", reached the town in 1828. It was this coach that later in the same year, carried to London the first issue of the Courier newspaper. By the 1830's there were no less than 45 well appointed stage coaches running to and from various towns. Large numbers of visitors flocked in - the not-so-rich by stage coach, the wealthy by their personal, finely-polished coach or carriage, the "Rolls-Royce" of the day.

(continued page 113)

The "Shakespeare" Coach, 1908, passing over the Avon Bridge, Warwick on it's return from Stratford-upon-Avon.

Listening to the band in the Pump Room Gardens, about 1900. Early perambulator.

Clemens Street. Funeral of Mr. Burgis, 5th November 1908.
Brewer's dray halted on left.

(left) Leisurely day on the Parade, about 1890. (Statue of
Queen Victoria did not appear until 1902.)

Delivery cart of George Welch, Butcher, 21 Bath Street, about 1900.

Mr. Dale's hackney cab and Mr. H. Gardner's Daimler Taxi outside G.W.R. Station, 1936. Station was then being rebuilt.

Rawlings and Winyard, Saddlers, 14 Clarendon Avenue, about 1910.

The following Livery Stables were established: Regent Hotel (capacity 100 horses, 50 carriages), Copps Royal Hotel (for 50 horses, 40 carriages), Probertts Orange Hotel (for 50 horses, 20-30 carriages), Clarendon Hotel, Crown Hotel, Warwick Tavern and Gloucester Mews. In 1851 those employed in the transportation business were:- coach builders and painters (46), coach guards etc. (25), cab proprietors, drivers and conductors etc. (33), horse-bus services (3), waggon drivers (3), carriers (3), leather makers, saddle and harness makers (21), blacksmiths, farriers, wheelwrights (59), horse breakers and dealers (4), ostlers, grooms, stable boys (several hundred) and many corn and fodder merchants.

There was also a thriving hire service in the town. Hopper said in 1842, "It never happens that every visitor brings his own chariot and pair to a public place, carriages therefore, in the best style, are provided of every description at stands (ranks) in every direction or ply for hire up and down the leading streets".

Rugby Road about 1920. Funeral of Mr. Donald, three times Mayor. Mr. Maynard drives leading carriage with the Borough Mace Bearer beside him.

It seems that the carriages were mainly phaetons but there were also flys, pony chaises and hacks. Other vehicles to appear were Broughams, Landaus, Victorias, Hansoms, waggonettes, brakes and light traps.

In those days short distances were often covered by horseback, Sedan chair or Bath chair. Apart from touring the town, visitors also travelled, generally by hired carriage, to see such historic places as Warwick and Kenilworth Castles, Stoneleigh, Guyscliffe and Charlecote. This was the "done thing" for all the newcomers. Visiting members of the aristocracy however, did not deign to join the tourist throngs but instead made their private arrangements for

(above) G.P.O. and Parish Church with cab rank and cabman's shelter, about 1904.

(left) Royal Pump Room, about 1904.

social calls on their titled equals. This was the case with the Hon. Mrs. Cavendish who, with her daughter, stayed at the Regent Hotel in 1832 for a month and spent most of her time visiting.

Around the 1840's many parties toured the district by pleasure coach using brakes (charabancs) and this surely was a most charming and effective way of seeing the sights and, on a nice summer's day, the lush green countryside as they bowled along the Warwickshire roads. Two well known local firms connected with the horse were the Bubb family who carried on a horse-breaking and horse-dealing business in Tavistock Street for more than a 100 years and Henry Mulliner who had 3 coach building works in the locality from about 1870 to 1888.

In the early 1900's when Leamington became a very popular "tripper resort Spa", there was a revival of pleasure coaching when two fine old coaches, the "Shakespeare" and the "Tally Ho", were given a new lease of life in providing excursions that departed daily from the Town Hall.

The Parade, about 1906.

Covent Garden Market about 1900. Delivery cart.

Victoria Park about 1920. Horse float in Hospital Carnival.

Workmen, each with his tool-of-trade, at premises of H . Savage, wheelwright, shoeing smith and general ironworker, 3 Court Street, about 1900. Mr E.F. "Dick" Smith stands fourth from right.

(right) Sidney Flavel's Eagle Foundry about 1850. Showing Flavel's boats on the canal.

THE CANAL

An essential contribution to the speedy development of the New Town north of the river during the period 1810-1840 was made by the existence of a new national transport system in the form of the canal commonly known as "the cut". The Warwick and Napton Canal, later part of the Grand Union network, passing through the southern part of Leamington, was opened for trade on 19th March, 1800, thus providing a direct connection with London and the industrial Midlands.

Leamington had to wait yet another 40 years or so before the railway reached it. Therefore the canal was a vital link with the outside world and soon became a very busy waterway. Right along from Tachbrook Road to Rushmore Street stretched a continuous line of active wharfs and warehouses, together with a loading basin at Clapham Street. The long cumbersome narrow boats ("barges"), drawn by towhorses plodding along the adjacent towpath, were slow but cheap and capable of carrying considerable loads. Because a large number of boats were always employed, speed really was not a problem. Thus Leamington received ample supplies of building materials, coal and heavy merchandise. It is assumed that most of the superb decorative ironwork on its many buildings had first made its way here from Midland foundries via the canal.

The Gas Works and canal about 1946.

Canal scene about 1910.

The canal and site of Gas Works, 1980.
The gas-holders were demolished 1982.

A rare instance of passenger-travel on the canal occurred in 1813 (or possibly 1814). The famous engineer William Murdock, while installing water-heating equipment at the Spa's Royal Pump Room, badly injured his leg and after a long spell of medical care, was finally transported by canal on an "excursion" boat to his home in Handsworth. This journey for the sick man was no doubt more comfortable than the alternative method by coach and its jolting along the rutted roads of that time!

"The Canal Boatman's Song" written at Leamington by James Bisset in 1816, conveys, in spite of its romantic nature, something of the atmosphere of working life on the canal. The lines of the second verse:-

> What tho' cramp'd for room, and pent
> In a cabin, where no vent
> Is found for black and noisome smoke?
> We gaily quaff and crack the joke;
> And as Brother Bargemen pass,
> Treat them with special glass;
> Or when village maids we 'spy
> Hail them as we're sailing by -
> Thus while months and seasons veer,
> Wearing out the motley year,
> Still content with humble cheer,
> Thus from port to port we steer,
> Singing ever blythe and free,
> What, tho' toilsome 'tis to me,
> Here no tyrant's slave you see,
> 'Tis a Life of Liberty!

The presence of the canal also brought about the early industrial growth in the area. The Gas Works were erected in 1819 close to the south bank in order to take advantage of the Grand Union canal for its supply of coal. Likewise Sidney Flavel began in 1833 his Eagle Foundry and, with his own fleet of narrow boats, utilised the waterway to bring in raw materials and transport out his finished products. In 1830 there were at least 4 carrier firms including Pickfords, operating locally – all from wharfs at Ranelagh Terrace, Ranelagh Street and Tachbrook Road. Bulk supplies of paper for the Courier were then delivered from London by canal. In 1836 publication was threatened because intense frost had stopped the passage of boats! In 1851 there were 21 men employed on the local canal but only 14 then engaged by the railay.

Towing-horses were gradually replaced by diesel-powered towboats, these being extensively used by the major carrier firm of Fellows, Moreton and Clayton Ltd., but even today we can still see signs of the towhorse days in the deep grooves worn by tow ropes into the corners of bridge arches along the local waterway.

Steam-driven narrow boats "President" and "Nantwich" approaching Leamington from Radford Semele, 1980.

The navigation canals, to use their proper name, were a great success and were at their height in the second half of the 19th century. There after began the long years of decline and neglect but today many waterways have been restored for recreational purposes and surviving narrow boats converted to pleasure craft.

Albion Row alongside canal, looking towards Clemens Street, 1957. Cottages demolished same year.

Bollard at top of steps (Clemens Street) leading down to canal tow path

THE IRON ROAD

The idea of using smooth iron rails as a "permanent way" for the passage of iron-wheeled waggons had distinct advantages. The most important feature was that there would not be the drag as experienced on road surfaces and, provided the track was level, very little energy was needed, once the initial inertia was overcome, to handle a considerable load. By about 1750 there were a number of short lines in use – generally these were in quarries and mines and trucks were often pulled by just a single horse. Such a line was the tram road linking Stratford-on-Avon with Moreton-in-the-Marsh; opened in 1826.

Little development took place until the historical introduction of steam traction for railways in 1814. Thus began the grand and glorious days of rail transport and within a few years vast rail systems had miraculously been opened up over the whole country with far-reaching effects on industrial and social life.

Leamington was not excluded and the rival lines of the L.M.S. and G.W.R. well and truly put it on the map and greatly influenced its role as a residential Spa. Since World War II

Official opening of the Leamington Passenger Terminus of the branch line from Coventry, December, 1844. The Station was at Rugby Road, Milverton (present Spinney estate).

Derailment of a mixed train while approaching Leamington, after passing Radford Brook, 1859. Three men were killed. From an original pencil sketch "took on spot" by Leamingtonian William Dawkes.

the rapid growth of road and air transport has taken away much of the business from the once prosperous railways and consequently large numbers of uneconomical local lines have been closed and other services reduced. Gone forever are many of the charming country lines with their flower bordered stations.

The story of the local tramway is limited to a term of half a century but it is not without its special interest and is, in a way, typical of the history of the tramway system in Britain. There were the pressing commercial problems, the fierce opposition, the development of horse and electric traction and the long, losing battle of competition with the motor bus.

Station Master's house associated with the 1844 Milverton Station, 1957. Both buildings constructed of blue brick and stone. The house was demolished in 1969.

The line between Leamington and Warwick was usually referred to by tram crews as "The Track" and even today there are those who use the same term to describe the bus service linking the two towns.

In the 1840's all over the country horse-drawn vehicles were steadily and irrevocably replaced by the Iron Horse of George Stephenson. Connected with the railways were turnpike roads and canals and these

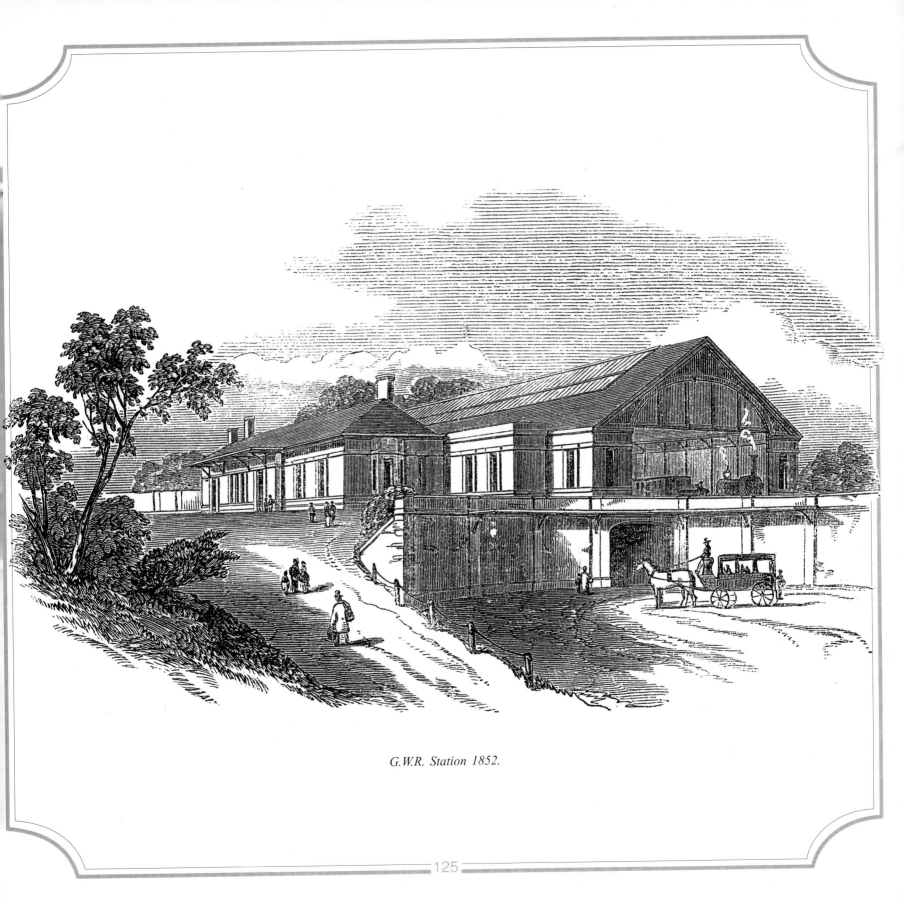

G.W.R. Station 1852.

G.W.R. Station about 1935.

Cabbies' chat-time, G.W.R. Station, about 1935.

Rebuilding of G.W.R. Station 1936-1938.

both contributed to cheap and rapid communications. The numerous railway systems were built by privately-owned companies which competed fiercely with each other for passenger and goods business. In the early years with regard to Leamington's role as a Spa, the coming of the railways was, after a promising beginning, a disappointment. Initially the trains brought large numbers of visitors but they soon shrank as the country's railways made it easier to travel to seaside resorts such as Brighton. Also the aristocracy were slow to adopt rail travel and preferred the door-to-door privacy and style of their own elegant horse-drawn carriages. The arrival in Leamington of the L.M.S. and G.W.R lines however eventually brought about the start of a new era for the town. Businessmen and workers were, for the first time, able to travel quickly and cheaply each day to the major Midland towns while at the same time an excellent heavy goods service was provided. The first local line, a branch from Coventry, reached Milverton in 1844. It was almost 9 miles long. The venture, although predicted a failure, proved to be very successful and in 1847 an extension was commenced to Avenue Road ("Avenue" Station) and on to Rugby.

Mick Hunt, standing far left, with workmates at G.W.R. Motive Power Depot (near Eagle Recreation Ground), about 1927.

5001 "Llandovery Castle" with express at G.W.R. Station 1931.

A high embankment and a lofty stone bridge over the river was constructed (present Princes Drive area) and to take the line to Rugby, another bridge was built across High Street. For this bridge the well-known buildings of Curtis's Baths and Copps Royal Hotel were demolished in 1847. The official opening of the extended line took place on 22nd February, 1851, followed by a banquet at the Regent Hotel.

Viaduct and New River Walk. Passenger train on the way to Coventry, about 1915.

Surprisingly the first station at Avenue Road was a poor affair being little more than a wooden shed. Due to public demand this was replaced by a new, extensive station, built in the Italian style and officially opened in March 1860. In 1964 passenger services between Coventry, Leamington and Rugby were discontinued and in 1968 Avenue Station and the track to Rugby were both dismantled. A garage now stands on the Station site. British Rail then rerouted the line from Coventry into Leamington ex-G.W.R Station and from 1977, in addition to goods trains, it also carried passenger trains when some of the Oxford-Birmingham Inter-City services started to run via Coventry. A few years after the opening of the

Entrance to Milverton Station, Warwick New Road, 1968 - year of demolition.

L.N.W.R. Coventry-Leamington line, steps were taken to complete the Birmingham and Oxford Junction Railway (later part of the G.W.R) under the supervision of Mr. I.K. Brunel, the famous railway engineer. This scheme would provide Leamington with a direct rail link with London and Birmingham. Construction activities locally commenced in 1851. Included were bridges on the Banbury side, a bridge across High Street and at Myton, an interesting aqueduct to carry the Grand Union Canal.

The site chosen for Leamington Station was on the Old Warwick Road, close to Avenue Station, which was occupied at the time by a partially-completed range of large terraced houses known as Eastnor Terrace. These houses were demolished and in their place the Station building was completed in 1852. It had, at the start, an all-over roof of Brunel's usual style as were the stations at Oxford and Banbury.

46446 with local passenger train arriving at Leamington (Milverton) Station, 1951.

L.M.S. Avenue Station, about 1910.

L.M.S. Avenue Station, 1951. Demolished 1968.

L.M.S. Avenue Station Railcar 1956.

To mark the opening of the new (broadgauge) line on the 30th September 1852, a large number of special guests started the inaugural journey from Paddington to Birmingham and finally to Leamington. However en-route they were beset by a chapter of accidents which delayed their arrival at the celebration banquet in the Regent Hotel by 2½ hours. The best of the food and wine had been consumed by that time by the other guests!

Excavation work during rebuilding of G.W.R. Station 1936-38.

In spite of a dismal inauguration the line was opened for passenger trains the following day on the 1st October 1852; the 129-mile journey from London to Birmingham being covered in a mere 2∫ hours. Goods traffic started in February, 1853. Brunel's 1852 Station building survived until its replacement by a splendid new one during 1936-38. The line continued to be very busy right up to the 1970's but after the modernization of the Euston-Coventry route, rail traffic through Leamington was drastically reduced and thus the station has now lost much of its earlier hustle and bustle.

Avenue Station signal box (L.M.S.) with G.W.R. box behind, 1967.

(left) 6660 hauling passenger train from Rugby and passing Radford Hall mansion, 1938.

THE LEAMINGTON AND WARWICK TRAMWAY

T o many people the idea of trams running between Leamington and Warwick must seem strange, yet for almost half a century they were part of the local scene - the first was horse-drawn, later electric. The last tram ran in 1930 and today there are many who have affectionate memories of their grinding, rattling sounds. This early form of public transport was never a great success locally but was well-suited for work and pleasure by the lower paid. It was very slow but reliable and cheap.

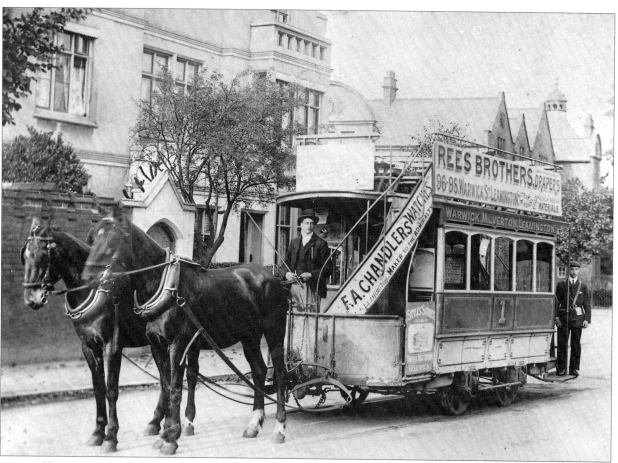

Horse tram No.1 at Station Approach, Avenue Terminus, about 1903. Public Library in background.

The horse-drawn tramway opened on 21st November, 1881 and closed on 16th May, 1905. The single-line track ran from a terminus at Station Approach, Avenue Road, up the Parade, along Warwick Street, through Emscote and up Smith Street to reach the Warwick terminus in High Street. The leisurely 3-mile journey took just under 40 minutes. Up to a maximum of 8 open-top double decker tramcars, each drawn by a pair of horses, were employed.

Horse tram No.7 at Station Approach, Avenue Road. George Powell driver,
Tommy Mumford conductor. About 1900.

When cars were heavily laden an extra "puller" horse was added to take the long steep gradients of the Parade, Emscote Road canal bridge and Smith Street/Eastgate. With stables at Coten End, the tramway had at one time as many as 45 horses.

Local folk nicknamed the trams "Wackrill and Bright's Rattlesnakes" after the two prominent local men who campaigned for their introduction. In August 1984 two sad-looking horse tramcars, long since retired, were rescued from Yarningale Common by the Birmingham Railway Museum - hopefully for restoration.

Proposals for the use of electric traction on the tramway were eventually accepted and, after major reconstruction, the first electric tram ran in July, 1905.

As the town was then dominated by horse-drawn traffic there was a great deal of suspicion and apprehension because of the high risk of horses being frightened by the rattles and the electric sparks of the new trams. They were however, very popular with visitors to the area during the Summer months.

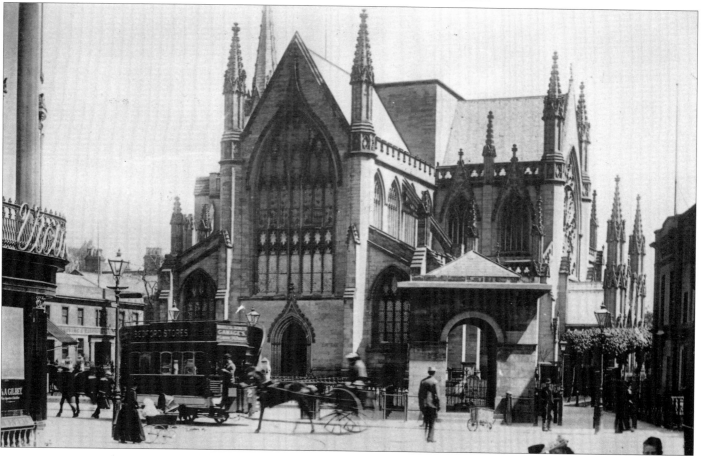

Horse tram in Victoria Terrace on its way to Warwick, 1892.

Rescue operation at Yarningale Common, August, 1984. Horse tram car No.1.

Comic cartoon portraying the hazards of travel by electric tram, 1905.

Horse tram with additional "puller" horse, rounds Eastgate, Warwick, about 1900.

The route was virtually as the old horse tramway, the single track of this being ripped up and replaced by twin tracks. At Emscote a small Power Station was specially constructed to supply the electricity. Each tram was to pick up its power from overhead wires and, to carry these lines, tall cast-iron columns were erected at the roadside except on the Parade, where they occupied the centre of the road. The tramcars were open-top double-deckers each painted in a livery of dark green and cream and providing seating for 22 (or 24) inside and 26 on the upper deck. In 1921 there were as many as 12 cars in use.

Electric tram car No. 1 at Avenue Road Terminus, about 1912.

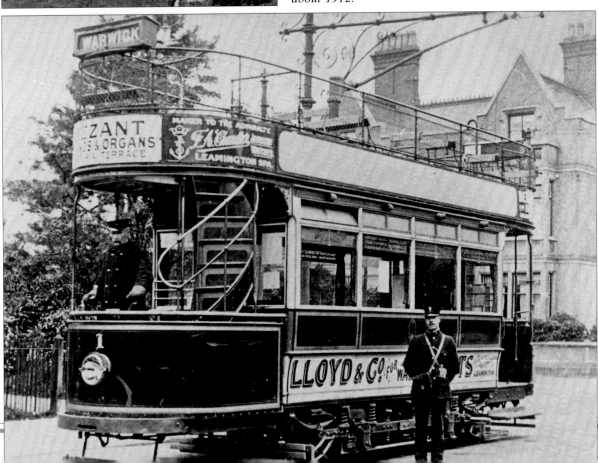

Trade mark of the British Electric Traction Co., on the base of a column in Avenue Road 1953. The column once supported the overhead power wires of the electric tramway.

By the late 1920's competition with the motor omnibuses became fierce, the struggle ending with defeat for the trams. The last passenger-carrying tram ran on 16th August, 1930.

It is probable that a solitary electric tram has survived to the present day - it was last reported to be at Colwyn Bay functioning as a stores shed.

Even though the trams ceased over 50 years ago their influence on the town remains to this day. The lamp columns running down the centre of the Parade are the modern counterparts of the first central columns ever to be erected in 1905 - these not only carried the tramway's overhead power wires but also each had a pair of ornate gas lamps attached.

(continued page143)

Electric tram arriving at Warwick Street from Warwick, about 1910.

Tram No. 6 moving down the Parade, about 1910.

(below) A view of Victoria Bridge showing a variety of transport, about 1910.

Tram opposite the Pump Room, about 1915.

Premises at No. 14 Parade, about 1920.

Tram from Warwick in Victoria Terrace, about 1920.

Tram car No. 2 on an otherwise empty Parade, about 1910.

Two electric trams in Victoria Terrace, about 1906.

THE MOTOR VEHICLE

When we look at the car-packed streets of modern Leamington it is difficult to realise that less than a hundred years ago there was not a single car to be seen. The pioneer days of mechanical road transport during the 1880's and 1890's produced all kinds of strange machines with a variety of means of propulsion such as steam, petrol and electricity. They were not generally welcomed in what was then a horse-drawn society and consequently severe and, by present standards, ludicrous restrictions were imposed on drivers. Even as late as 1896 the law required that all self-propelled vehicles on the road had a man walking in front with a red flag and the speed limit to be 4mph, but after this date conditions eased slightly when the man and flag was no longer needed and the speed limit raised to 14mph. The first cars in Leamington appeared in very few numbers in the early 1890's and there were still only a handful in 1910. The newfangled devices were regarded by many as dangerous, unsavoury things and, being expensive, were initially owned only by the nobility, the wealthy and a few professional people. Lesser mortals were filled with awe and admiration as they watched the rich folk purring along in their glittering Daimlers in superior contempt for those still struggling with horse-drawn carriages.

3.5 H.P. Benz, first privately - owned motor car in Leamington; belonging to Miss Gowen. The machine, driven by Mr. Tom Thacker, was first seen in the town in 1896.

An early indication that the motor vehicle had indeed come to stay was the Motor Car Act of 1903 which first introduced registration of all mechanical road vehicles both passenger and goods. The first manufacture of cars on a grand scale was commenced in 1909 by Henry Ford in the U.S.A., with mass-production of his Model T "Tin Lizzie". These cars and vans were soon a common sight in Leamington. Between 1910 and 1925 there was considerable development so that by the early 1920's there were, in Leamington, about six major garages, these having commenced by hiring out cars and later becoming sales agencies for popular makes such as Austin, Morris,

Motor hackney cabs waiting on the Parade rank about 1910.

Ford, Rover, Riley, Daimler, Humber, Sunbeam, Citroen and Darracq. During the interwar years the streets of the town became increasingly occupied by cars and motor cycles though, as yet, they had by no means completely replaced horse-drawn vehicles.

A halt to the trend came during and just after World War II when new cars were almost unobtainable and bicycles then ruled the roads. From the 1950's followed the first great boom in the motor industry when large quantities of small family cars like the Mini, Morris Minor, Ford Popular and Hillman Imp were produced. Nowadays the motor car has become not so much a rich man's luxury but rather a necessity of modern living and thus now dominates the town scene. For many however, public transport continues to be a convenient alternative form of conveyance. From 1905 to 1935 there was considerable growth, with

(right) Vintage car, Reg. No. AA 573 in Tachbrook Road, about 1950.
(below) A motor car, a carriage and a Bath chair on the Parade, about 1912.

Lower Parade with Tilling - Stevens Midland Red bus and bull-nose Morris, about 1925.

fierce competition, in local bus services including the Stratford Blue (1927) and the Leamington and Warwick Green Buses (1928). All the small companies were finally taken over in 1935 by the Birmingham bus company later to be known as the Midland Red. The history of the bicycle is lengthy but most important was the invention by James Starley of the "Safety Bicycle" in Coventry during the 1870's. Cycling soon became popular and by 1883 there were in the town 7 Bicycle and Tricycle Depots. After the turn of the century there began the new health craze of "Bicycle Mania" and after passing through several other successful phases, has now become a part of daily life.

Evolving from the bicycle the motor cycle began to appear during the period 1880-1900 and really came into its own in the war years of 1914-1918, continuing to enjoy great favour right up to the 1950's.

The Parade about 1925 with less than 12 cars in sight.

Midland Red double-decker bus in Warwick Street, 1970.

Midland Red bus, 1925.

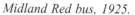

One of the Borough's last steam rollers, in Clarendon Place, about 1950.

(below) Warwickshire County Council steam waggon AC 65, about 1920.

(left) Traffic build-up in Bath Street, 1976.

Traffic chaos at High Street - Tachbrook Road junction 1973.

(above) Cars everywhere. Regent Grove 1962.

LETTER AND THE LAW

INTRODUCTION

The work of the Police, in all its varied aspects, is unfortunately rather taken for granted but nevertheless is of prime importance to the life of the town today. Without their presence conditions would be chaotic.

As Leamington developed from a humble village to a splendid Spa, the Police Force similarly evolved and grew accordingly and its history, over more than 150 years, makes a fascinating study. The Police have always been available for emergencies of all kinds and also for the prevention and detection of crime. There are without doubt many older residents today who can clearly remember the familiar figures of the local bobbies in the 1930's. Long before the introduction of patrol cars it was a common sight in the town to see policemen either on the beat or directing traffic or even in their alternative role as firemen in the Police Fire Brigade.

The local policeman was always around and ready to give a hand in times of trouble and, as many will recall, available to deliver a stern warning or a "cuff round the ear" to the troublesome lads of the town.

In the very early days crime was generally of a minor nature - such as flying a kite before 8 a.m. – but in modern times the increased amount and severity of crime places a heavy burden on those responsible for law and order.

We rarely give the Postal Service a second thought except perhaps when late deliveries or rising prices become the subject of local protests. Even so the Post Office provides a vital communication system today for the people of Leamington. For more than 200 years the local service has sought to keep pace with the needs of an ever-increasing population.

The postmen in Leamington no longer collect the mail on street corners with the aid of a handbell but he (or she) continues to provide a valuable daily door-to-door delivery of mail. The extensive use of the telephone nowadays has, to a degree, made letters unnecessary but undoubtedly the Postal Service still retains a key role in today's commerce and in the lives of private residents.

Green Farm viewed from Church Green, Whitnash c.1900

The Police (and Fire Brigade)

T he early history of the local Police is rather bewildering but it is hoped that the following details will serve to give a fairly clear description.

There were three authorities involved, each of them appointing their own officers – either constables, watchmen or street-keepers. It is not surprising that there was a great deal

The Leamington Borough Police Force proudly pose on the steps of the Police Station, High Street, on the occasion of Queen Victoria's Diamond Jubilee on 22nd. June, 1897. Each officer, complete with fearsome spiked helmet, is wearing his Jubilee medal.

of confusion in those formative years. The three authorities were: -

a)	the Parish Committee;
b)	the County Magistrates;
c)	the Town Improvement Commissioners.

The first authority, the Parish Committee, was the old constitutional form of parochial government under which the affairs of the village had been controlled for centuries. The Committee was appointed annually by the Vestry and acted as a governing body responsible for the management of the parish business. They had comprehensive powers and enjoyed an important social status; all secular affairs in the town were in their care. The town's earliest police force was selected and controlled by the Parish Committee and up to 1825 consisted, of two constables (one being the superior officer), one head borough (sometimes none or even up to three), a third borough (sometimes none or even two), and a pinner and crier - who was also sworn in as an assistant constable. The two constables were paid about ten shillings a week. William Langham was the earliest principal constable, (1824). In 1825 the two officers were George Reading and John Hickling.

THE PARISH FIRE SERVICE

For hundreds of years fire-fighting in the humble village of Leamington Priors had not been an organised affair and was limited to the application of pails of water carried by hand.

As the new Spa grew, it soon became obvious that some kind of fire extinguishing appliance was required and thus, possibly around 1810-1820, the Parish Committee introduced a manual fire pump which was kept in a building erected in a part of the old parish churchyard.

During 1825 considerable improvements were made to the fire service and also a new local law was

A painted stone model of a late 18th century manual fire pump, with helmeted firemen as supporters. It was the trade mark of the Birmingham Fire Office, a fire insurance company. The group stands over the entrance of Locke and England, 1 and 2 Euston Place having been sited before over the porch of their earlier premises at 166, the Parade. An authentic pump of a similar type is today on display at the Warwickshire Fire Brigade H.Q., in Warwick Street. It was made by Stock and Taylor, Birmingham, around 1770 and was previously at Packington Hall.

established which prohibited the use of thatch on all new buildings.

The second authority was the County Magistrates who, in 1824, created a rather impractical dual system of policing. They decided that the Parish Committee should no longer have the sole appointing power regarding the police but rather that they, the County, should also have this authority. A number of important townspeople had complained that the force run by the Parish was insufficient for the growing town and, as a result, the County set up a separate policing force on December 8th, 1824, by swearing in four watchmen of their own to patrol the Leamington streets. This was the first-ever departure from the old parochial system

The Shand Mason Steamer fire engine "Victoria" makes a stirring sight at a Police Fire Brigade demonstration in the Victoria Park 28th. September, 1901. The Steamer was retained until 1925.

and may be regarded as the time when the foundation was laid of the Leamington Borough Police Force. (Note that this was nearly five years earlier than the founding of the renowned Metropolitan Police Force by Sir Robert Peel in 1829.)

At this time most of the local matters dealt with concerned trouble at night, late drinking and the opening of shops on a Sunday. Unfortunately the early Parish officers were not always trustworthy. One man was reported for being drunk in the town and causing a disturbance. He kept his post on promise of good behaviour but was subsequently dismissed for a further bout of drunkenness when "he had from negligence suffered a man under a charge of felony to escape"! The Parish Committee at one time purchased a "strait waistcoat" for the use of the parish and also supplied the town with stocks (possibly erected in High Street).

The third authority was the Town Improvement Commissioners. This new form of local government was created by an 1825 Act of Parliament which provided for "properly paving and stoning, gravelling or flagging, cleansing, lighting and watching (policing), regulating and improving the town, also preventing nuisances in the streets and on the footpaths". Among those nuisances considered illegal and punishable by fines up to £5, were "the act of obstructing a passage by playing marbles or hoops, exposing stallions, letting certain dogs go at large unmuzzled, driving horses furiously, carrying animal carcases without sufficient covering, putting out flowerpot not sufficiently guarded, wanton knocking of doors and flying kites and beating rugs before 8 a.m.

The Steamer fire engine "Victoria" passing over the Victoria Bridge as part of a procession for the Warneford Hospital Gymkhana. The St. John's ambulance follows behind, with the tall figure of Chief Constable T. T. Earnshaw, in plain clothes, on its right. About 1910.

The brass-helmeted volunteer Fire Brigade pose in front of "Victoria" steamer fire engine at the Althorpe Street Fire Station, about 1900. Note the engine's large brass chimney. Captain of the brigade was Mr. McWilliam.

As if it was not confusing enough already (by having a police force controlled by two separate authorities), the Commissioners decided to also enter into local police affairs! Therefore, as certain police powers had been conferred on them by the 1825 Act, the Commissioners established their own, quite separate, police force for "abating nuisances to inhabitants". The first Head Constable was John Palmer (salary £150 p.a.). The new constables (pay 15/- weekly), were empowered to "use their utmost endeavours to prevent mischief and misdemeanour". They could arrest and detain "all felons and loose, idle and disorderly persons disturbing the peace and loitering

(left) Motor Fire Tender Regn. No. AC 184, 1903. Designed and built in Leamington by Charles T. Crowden.

The Borough Police stand at ease outside the Town Hall, about 1910. Parade shops shown are Andrew, Son and Co., Lucas and Co. and B. Rogers Knight. The lethal-looking spikes on the helmets were discontinued sometime before 1920

in the street between sunset and eight in the morning. Anyone damaging the new street lamps provided for in the 1825 Act could be seized by any other persons and taken before a J.P. where, upon conviction, they faced a fine of not more than £5 plus damages". If the offender refused to, or could not pay, he faced one month's hard labour in the "Common Gaol".

Thus from 1825 and up to 1839, the disjointed business of maintaining law and order somehow managed to function. It was just as well that in those days the peace of the town was not difficult to keep!

By 1839 the Commissioners' police force had grown to an impressive size of 16 members, the Head Constable then being William Shirley Roby with an annual salary of £150.

The year 1839 was to introduce controversial complications into the already complex local policing system. Sir Robert Peel's Constabulary Act was passed in this year and, as a result, the policing of the town became the responsibility of the County Constabulary. Strangely, there seemed to have been no demand by the County that the Town Commissioners should now disband their own police force. Even so, to the townspeople it was assumed at first that the existing Force would in fact be swallowed up by the County because of various proposals made by the Commissioners. They had suggested that they were willing to relinquish their control of the Force on condition that their Head Constable, William Roby, was appointed Chief Constable of the County and that Leamington be made the headquarters of the Knightlow Hundred. As an inducement to the Court of County Quarter

Leamington Borough Police items worn by P.C. Fred Cater: the large distinctive helmet plate featuring the Royal Coat-of-Arms, shoulder-piece bearing the Borough Coat-of-Arms, a tunic button and belt buckle. The helmet plates were replaced by a new design and the shoulder-pieces discontinued about 1936.

Sessions to acquiesce to this proposal, they offered the free use of the Police Headquarters (a large room, offices, cells etc.) currently in use in part of the (old) Town Hall, High Street. The County declined these proposals and instead decided to advertise for candidates for the post of County Chief Constable and eventually out of 11 applicants; including Leamington's Mr. Roby, the choice fell on Capt. George Baker, R.N. He thus became, in 1840, the County's first Chief Constable and, in effect, the third for Leamington. Almost at once it became clear to the Town Commissioners that the County arrangements for Leamington were pitifully inadequate. The plan was that Leamington would share, with seven other parishes, a grand total of only seven policemen i.e. a share-out of less than one constable per parish. This meant that the County Constabulary presence in the town consisted of $\frac{7}{8}$'s of one policeman and for this pathetic service the town had to pay, on average, a police rate of £500. Fortunately, as the County had rejected the Commissioners 1839 proposal, the Commissioners had retained their own force and when the County's arrangements became known, it was considered advisable to still keep the old force - though on a reduced scale and with a new title. William Roby, Head Constable, was appointed Town Surveyor and to give him suitable authority, the Parish

Police Sergeant No.4 and Chief Constable T.T. Earnshaw on duty during the visit of the Duke of York (later King George VI) to the Pump Room, 3rd. June, 1924. The Mayor was George W. Hawkins.

Vestry made him also parish constable. Several of the former policemen were retained as street-keepers with duties not clearly defined. These local arrangements were regarded by the County Chief Constable (Capt. Baker) as irregular and interfering with matters under his authority and, from then on, constant and bitter bickering arose between the two police forces - hardly a good example by the custodians of civil law and order! The situation became absurd. The Leamington street-keepers turned up their noses at the County Constable and he, in return, looked down on them with an air of lofty contempt. Capt. Baker declined to acknowledge Mr. Roby who, trusting to his Vestry appointment, considered

Racing off from Althorpe Street Fire Station to answer a call, about 1925. The Leyland engine, Regd. No. NX 8789 (2nd. June 1925), was probably "The Queen". The Fire Station was located in the arches of the railway bridge.

himself quite as good as the Captain. When chancing to meet on the Parade they coldly ignored one another; one of them usually deciding to cross to the other side of the road or perhaps stopping and turning his back, to gaze at some "compelling" display in a shop window.

Even the Town Commissioners joined in the conflict by refusing the County the use of the local police head quarters in the (old) Town Hall. They did, however, offer the Police Sub-Station at 17 Park Street. Capt. Baker accepted this but following his refusal to pay the rent, the Commissioners gave him notice to quit! It soon became clear that such a ludicrous state of affairs could not possibly be allowed to continue and, in order to settle things, a large Committee consisting of the Town Commissioners and other principal residents and tradesmen, met together to prepare a new and more comprehensive local Act which would include the vexed matter of the police establishment. The earlier 1825 Act was no longer sufficient for the town's needs.

At long last in 1843 the confused problem of policing Leamington was resolved when the new local Act was passed on June 27th of that year. It empowered the Commissioners

Leyland fire engine "The Queen" with Chief Constable T.T.Earnshaw in plain clothes, about 1925 - the year the engine was bought. Purchased by the Lockheed factory in 1939, it remained the work's first-line appliance until about the 1960's. It is now in a Lincolnshire preservation museum. Its predecessor "The King"; the 1914 Leyland, was kept by the Leamington Fire Brigade until 1945. The fate of "The King" is obscure but it is believed that it went to a Coventry breaker's yard and, in more recent years, that it is undergoing restoration in Cambridgeshire.

The Police leaving the Parish Church after a service and possibly on the way to the War Memorial on Remembrance Sunday in the early 1930's. In the picture are Chief Constable T.T. Earnshaw, Sgt. Moore, Sgt. W. Jones and P.C. A.J. Morris.

once again to establish their own police force. A Police Committee was appointed and in the August of 1843 they reported having reinstated Mr. W.S. Roby as head of the new police force at a salary of £135 p.a. The 10 constables received £1 per week each, subject to a deduction of 2/- weekly for clothing and 1/- a week to "create a sick fund". As a sense of order finally replaced chaos, the way was now clear for the firm establishment and steady expansion of the Leamington Police Force. Head of Police, Mr. Roby, was eventually followed by Mr. J. Thompson. April 1859 saw the retirement of Mr. Thompson and, out of 35 applicants, Mr. John Lund, who had previously served 23 years in the Metropolitan Police and then retired on a pension, was selected as Superintendent of Police and Inspector of Nuisances (he served in this capacity until retirement in 1881).

A Voluntary Fire Brigade was formed by Lund in 1863 and he then took over the additional responsibility of Captain of the Brigade, while a police sergeant became leading fireman. Almost all of the volunteers were men employed in the building trade; their knowledge being a valuable asset when fighting fires. Three manual engines were kept at the rear of the (old) Town Hall in High Street and were garaged under the arches of the nearby railway bridge. Additional, smaller fire substations were later established in Chandos Street, Union Road and in Cubbington Road, Lillington. The Fire Brigade continued on a voluntary basis until 1900 when a full-time service was introduced. The Chief Constable (Mr. Alex Thompson), then also became the Fire Brigade Chief Officer and half of the current strength (40) of the Borough Police were appointed to perform the alternative task of firemen as and when the need arose. At this time one of the engines was a Shand Mason "Steamer" drawn by two powerful horses. Horses were borrowed from the Chapel Street works of Kinmonds, manufacturers of aerated waters. This appliance was actually a large upright, coal-fired boiler which produced steam to drive the water pumps feeding the fire hoses. It was retained at the Fire Station as late as January, 1925.

Leamington Police Station, High Street, about 1946. Building was originally the first Town Hall (1831) and is today the Polish Club.

In 1903 the Brigade took delivery of a new Motor Fire Tender which had been specially designed and built for the Borough by Charles T. Crowden at his Packington Place Works, Leamington. This vehicle was indeed a modern innovation and the first of its type in this country – where transport was still predominantly horse-drawn. Most of the Police firemen lived in nearby George Street and each of their houses was fitted with an electric bell which was operated from the Police Station when a fire alarm was raised.

(below) The Borough Police stand for inspection, with T.T. Earnshaw, at the Drill Hall, Adelaide Road, probably on Silver Jubilee Day (King George V), 1935. Inspector J.W. Grooby nearest, front row.

(left) The town's Blue Lamp outside the High Street Police Station, with George Street in the background, 1954. The lantern had blue and white panels reading "Police" on three of its sides. It was, at first, one of a pair of unmarked lamps which were mounted on two pillars when the building was opened as the Town Hall in 1831. This lamp is now in the Leamington Art Gallery and Museum.

(left) *Marching out of the Police Station about 1937 - note the white gloves. Each evening a column of men departed from the Station to commence a night's spell of duty on the beat. As they proceeded up the town, the men detached themselves from the column to commence their own allotted beat. Average walking distance for a night beat was between 20 and 25 miles. The picture shows P.C.F. Cater, P.C.R. Bailey, P.C.C. Manley and Sgt. J. Edgington.*

(right) *Silver Jubilee Day, 1935, outside the Town Hall. Included in the photograph are T.T. Earnshaw, P.C.s Sid Shuff, Jim Green, Alf J. Morris and G. Gibbs.*

Sgt. A. Pitcher, Insp. J.W. Grooby and Chief Constable T.T. Earnshaw receive their Silver Jubilee medals from Dr.H. Mason, 1935. Mr. Earnshaw had already got the 1911 Coronation medal.

AMBULANCE SERVICE

In the early days, possibly from about 1900, the Police, in addition to their already varied duties as policemen and firemen, also had to maintain an ambulance service. The first conveyances used were hand carts which bore a flat, wicker-edged "bed" and it is known that these were still operated up to about 1930; particularly for first aid at the popular annual Gymkhanas in the Victoria Park. It is probable that the service was later improved by the introduction of a horse-drawn ambulance. From 1902, on the instruction of Chief Constable T.T. Earnshaw, all constables were required to attend St. John's Ambulance classes to qualify in first aid for the injured.

The last sad days of the Borough Police Force. A photograph of the final get-together on the steps of the Police Station in 1947, the year the Borough Force was brought to an end and the Warwickshire Constabulary took over. The front row consists of members of the police watch committee with Chief Constable. W. Rees sitting next to the Mayor, Ald. Oswald R. Davidson.

Up to 1884 the Police had occupied just one portion of the High Street Town Hall but once the new Town Hall on the Parade was opened in that year, they took over the entire High Street building which was then renamed the Police Station.

Chief Constable Thomas Taylor Earnshaw took office in 1902, having previously been Police Superintendent at Wigan. He continued as Leamington's Chief Constable until 1938, the year that he died, aged 68. Over the 36 years Mr. Earnshaw became a very well-known and respected personality in the town and was never absent from important events. Succeeding Chief Constables were: - J.H. Hanlon (1938-39), Arthur Young (1939-41), Mr. Martin (1941-42), W. Rees (1943-47).

The Special Constabulary first started in Leamington in 1914 at the outbreak of the first World War, after Chief Constable Earnshaw published an appeal in the Courier 28th August 1914 for public spirited men to join the new Leamington voluntary force. Thirty-five were sworn in the next morning. Among the early Specials were G. Bradford, H.J. Dawson, Arnold Thornton, P.H. Woodward and Councillor R.S. Salt. Ever since the "Specials" have played a valuable part in local police work.

FIRE SERVICE

The Borough Fire Brigade continued on a steady course until 1937. With the growing threat of a second World War, massive emergency plans were set in motion. Leamington Borough initiated the forming of a local brigade of the Auxiliary Fire Service and 50 firemen were enrolled. On the 18th August, 1941, all fire brigades were nationalised and in Leamington the office of Chief Fire Officer ceased and the town's police fire brigade then became part of Region No. 9 of the National Fire Service. Several members of the original brigade were retained as full-time firemen while others chose to continue their service in wholly police duties.

In 1948 the Warwickshire County Fire Brigade came into being and their splendid new Headquarters in Warwick Street was opened on 18th July, 1962.

The Leamington Police Force had grown steadily over the years and the following figures (total strength) serve to demonstrate this: 1843 (11), 1874 (23), 1890 (41), 1947 (about 55).

The 1946 Police Act sounded the death knell of the long-lived and much respected Borough Police Force which sadly ended its life on 1st April, 1947 and thus passed into the realm of town history, while its men lost their local identity and became just additional numbers to the already large strength of the Warwickshire Constabulary. The County had finally succeeded where they had virtually failed in 1839 and totally failed in 1843.

A familiar institution and a closely-knit team vanished in a moment and with it went a way of life that its members had grown accustomed to with the passage of time. The men suffered a sudden blow as so many of them had given long years of loyal and devoted service to their own Special Force - one which had always been closely associated with the life of the community.

Inspector Glynn Evans (Borough Police 1936-47) said this at the time: "To say we had lost interest would be to put it mildly. With a few exceptions we were almost rebellious and almost overnight, what was a highly efficient and interested body of men became sullen, bored bobbies!!" Most of the men were dispersed around the County while others departed to seek promotion in other areas. At the same time a Leamington Division of the County Force, headed by Superintendent J.C. Gardner, was established in the town. Constable Harry Hughes retired from the County Force in September, 1976. He was the last serving policeman of those who were originally in the Borough Force - which he had joined in 1946.

POST OFFICE

With major changes in the postal service taking place in recent years - and yet more to come – it is interesting to note that just over a hundred years ago the people of Leamington were asking whether they could expect an improvement in the postal facilities of the town, not because of reorganisation but because of the opening of a fine new Post Office at Priory Terrace. In particular they were hoping that morning deliveries to the outskirts of the town would be received by 10 a.m. The new Post Office, built at a cost of £2,300 excluding the fittings, opened on March 20th 1870 and replaced the building at Bath Street which had been used since about 1834. The addition of a ponderous porch to the old building in 1846 did little to lighten the interior and was described as dark, stuffy and cramped. Even so, Sidney Flavel, showed a proper appreciation for the imposing appearance of the portico because, when it was demolished in 1871, he bought the Doric columns to erect at his residence, then known as Edgeville House in Newbold Terrace, where they can still be seen.

The postal history of any town is an interesting study embracing early buildings, transport and the individuals connected with it. Leamington is fortunate in that its first Postmaster, Ben Satchwell (1732-1810), was a character who more than most stamped his personality on the town. Renowned as the man whose vision first saw the financial benefit mineral springs could bring to the backward little village, his part-time activity from 1783 as Postmaster is less well known. Yet his shabby, thatched cottage which stood at the bottom of New Street was the first post office to serve Leamington Priors, a parish of about twenty thatched houses. Ben combined his postal duties with his trade as boot and shoe maker. In his shop window a pane of glass had been removed and replaced with a little, black door about 10 inches wide and 14 inches high, with a tiny knocker. To post a letter, one rapped the knocker, the door was opened and the letter taken in. Postal charges then were paid by the recipient of the letter not the sender - thus it was very much in the interest of the Post Office that mail was properly delivered!

Isaac Bloomfield was appointed Leamington's first letter-carrier in 1817 and was the only one for several years. In those days he used to ride every day on horseback, armed with a regulation sword and a brace of pistols, to the Woolpack Hotel, Warwick. There he delivered the outgoing mailbag and collected any items addressed to Leamington. On his return he rang a small handbell to announce the arrival of the mail in the village. At that time a score of letters was considered a heavy delivery! Isaac was a rather tall, portly man with a marked

Leamington's first Post Office (1783), at Ben Satchwell's thatched cottage at the end of Mill Street. At this time it served only about 20 houses.

Benjamin Satchwell who became the first Postmaster in 1783. A popular man with many talents, he combined the postal business with his trade as boot-maker. He turned his lively mind to reading and writing and was much respected as a "poor-man's lawyer". Without doubt Ben was a founder of modern Leamington because his vision and enterprise was responsible for the development of the village into an elegant and fashionable Spa. He also acted as unofficial publicity agent often sending copies of his own verses to Coventry and London newspapers praising the Spa.

military bearing (he had been in the Army) and was nicknamed "The Major". His manner was hearty and genial and he always had a kind word and a joke for everybody. Following the death of Ben Satchwell in 1810, Elizabeth his daughter became Post-mistress but on marrying Richard Hopton the business was transferred to her husband. Hopton ran the town's first boarding house in Satchwell Place quite close to Satchwell's old cottage.

A local guide of the time describes the Post Office at Ben's residence as "very conveniently situated about 200 yards east of the church, with pretty adjoining gardens for the accommodation of visitors waiting for letters. A row of houses was built by old Satchwell [Elizabeth Satchwell] from this spot to Gordon House and called, after him, Satchwell Place. Here, visitors waiting for letters may promenade".

What a delightful, leisurely picture of early Regency Leamington this conjures up!

In 1816 Satchwell Place and "the thatched cottage lately occupied as the Post Office" was advertised to let. Richard Hopton had sold his boarding house and moved to Clemens Street and it is possible that the postal business was continued there.

The town was growing fast. The popularity of its spa waters drew ever-increasing numbers of visitors and the postal business increased accordingly. The first improvements to the service since Satchwell's day came in 1818 when, due to the exertions of Mr. Charles Mills (M.P. for Warwick), the town was given its first direct Royal Mail Coach link to London. As a result letters were then delivered in Leamington between 9 and 10 o'clock in the morning and replies could be posted up to 4 o'clock. Shortly after this came what is possibly the first recorded offence against a letter box in this country when on the 13th August, 1824 some "evil disposed" person threw a lighted cracker into the letter box at the Leamington Post Office. Three days later a poster appeared offering a 2 guineas reward for his apprehension.

(left) Bath Street as it appeared in 1846. The Post Office was then situated in the building with the large portico, on the right. The Royal Coat-of-Arms is proudly displayed on the balcony.

(left) Postman Frederick ("Freddy") Smith, in 1862.

(right) Postman Frederick Smith at his retirement in 1900, after 46 years in the postal service.

About this time great dissatisfaction was felt by the public who considered that in the fast-growing town, it was not really good enough to have the postal service run simply as a sideline for a tradesman. Agitation for a separate Post Office increased. It was finally successful and in mid-February, 1830 the new Post Office was opened at 36 Bath Street (Now No. 29) with George Bevington as Postmaster.

Three years later he was succeeded by the long-serving Edward Enoch and the Post Office was transferred to his premises (now No. 43 Bath Street). Only part of his boot and shoe shop was used for postal business and entry to it was by a very narrow doorway. The method of delivering mail up to 1830 was by a messenger standing on a street corner ringing his bell to summon the inhabitants to collect their letters. One cannot help but feel a touch of nostalgia when reading of the old ways - though the job itself must have been grim on a wet and windy day - but what is conveyed most forcibly is how quiet life must have been to hear the sound of the postman's bell some distance away and within the four walls of one's house. In 1833 there were two letter-carriers - Isaac Bloomfield and Samuel Hunt but in 1836, due to the town's rapid growth, George Abbotts was also taken on.

As the New Town continued to develop, the Post Office engaged a letter-carrier to go round the remote parts of the town in the evening with a bell collecting letters. He was "Old Joe Mallard" who carried out this task from 1840 to about 1870. A rather taciturn individual, he carried a supply of stamps to oblige his customers and he was so punctual with his bell that he was said to be as reliable as the church clock. The use of a handbell ceased about 1870, although Mallard remained in the postal service until 1879. The bell he used is still on

2 GUINEAS REWARD.

WHEREAS some evil-disposed PERSON or PERSONS, did, on the Night of the 13th instant, between the hours of Eleven and Twelve o'Clock, put

A Lighted Cracker

INTO THE LETTER-BOX.

BELONGING TO THE

Post-Office of Leamington,

A REWARD of TWO GUINEAS will be given on conviction, to any one who will give Information (at the POST-OFFICE,) of the Person or Persons who committed the Offence, that he or they may be Punished according to the utmost rigour of the Law.

(By Command of the Post-Master-General.)

B. CHURCHILL, *Surveyor,*

G. P. O.

Leamington Spa, Aug. 16, 1824.

ROSE & LAPWORTH, PRINTERS, CLEMEN'S STREET, LEAMINGTON.

(left) An event which took place on the night of 13th August, 1824, gave Leamington a rather unusual claim to fame. It is possibly the earliest recorded offence against a letter box in this country. The poster offers a reward of 2 guineas for information leading to the conviction of an "ill-disposed" person who dropped a lighted firecracker into the letter box of the Leamington Post Office.

view in the Leamington Art Gallery and Museum.

The American novelist Nathaniel Hawthorne stayed in Leamington in 1857 and recorded his memories in his book "Our Old Home". In it he refers to "the red-coated postman who went his rounds twice a day to deliver letters and again in the evening, ringing a handbell to take letters for the mail". When Rowland Hill introduced the Penny Post system in 1839 business in Leamington increased by a third. This necessitated alterations being made to the premises (which became the present 41 and 43 Bath Street) and the erection of the portico in 1846. At the same time new uniforms were provided by the public for post office officials - blue coat and vest, scarlet collar and cuffs with a gold band round the hat emulating the uniform of the Metropolitan postmen. There was a great and slavish admiration in Leamington at that time for anything which originated in the Capital. In 1846 the number of letters handled weekly was 40,000 which grew to 200,000 by 1901 and handled by a staff of 180. On 1st February, 1904 the first motorized service for distribution of parcels in the area was introduced. The van started from Warwick about 9 a.m., calling at Leamington to load, and then to Kenilworth, Coventry and Birmingham, returning to Warwick between 4 and 5 p.m.

(right) Old Joe Mallard, the last of the town's letter-carriers whose job, up to about 1870, was to walk to outlying parts of the town and ring a handbell, thus calling residents to bring out their letters for posting.

(above) The 1870 Head Post Office at Priory Terrace about 1910. Postmen and telegram messenger boys enjoy a chat in the sun. On the left is part of the lovely old chestnut tree which survived until 1985. Found to be badly decayed, it was sadly felled 2nd July.

(left) A postman in his shako helmet, on a delivery round in the Lower Parade, early one summer morning, about 1900. Note the heavily shuttered shop windows and the absence of Queen Victoria's statue.

The postal counter at the Head Post Office, Priory Terrace closed in March, 1971 and reopened at a new branch office in Victoria Terrace where it remained until December, 1978. It then returned to its former home in Priory Terrace. The Head Office building in the early 1970's was planned for demolition; to make way for a new Post Office, but happily the proposal was abandoned mainly due to economy. Instead the elegant 1870 building was redeveloped and extended during 1975-78 and became fully operational in December 1978. The formal opening took place on 18th January, 1979. Leamington's growth is well illustrated by the increase in postal business over the years. A staff of 3 had grown to 12 in 1851, 20 in 1871 and, early in 1986, the total postal staff had reached 236 of which 154 were postmen/postwomen. The present

(continued page180)

More than 30 postmen, with clerks and telegram messenger boys, make a fine group outside the Head Post Office, about 1906. Mr. F.T. Woodward is pictured far right of second row from front, he was postal Inspector 1906-15.

(left) A Ford Model 'T' Royal Mail van, about 1915.

The ladies take over. Post Office staff about 1915, when all deliveries, including telegrams, were carried out by women who each did two daily journeys on foot. At this time women had taken over most jobs while the men were away in the 1914-18 war. The man on the left, in flat cap, is Mr. Worrall, Postmaster, and next to him is believed to be Mr. F.T. Woodward, Inspector. Mrs. Alice Archer is far left on second row from the front. Also pictured are Mrs. Wiggins, Mrs. Hyde, Mrs. Whelan and Mrs. Varney

G.P.O. Staff Home Guard, during Second World War.

Building previously the Parade Branch Post Office, 47 Parade, advertised for sale, 1956. The office moved from here to 17 the Parade sometime between 1953 and 1956.

(left) Victorian pillar box in Binswood Street, April 1957. All the buildings on the right, including Clarendon House, were demolished about 1960. The box has since gone.

(right) Victorian pillar box in Leicester Lane, April, 1957 which was originally at Burton Dassett and finally removed from Leicester Lane about 1958. Box is of the Penfold type (1866-79) and was made by Cochrane Grove & Co.

The first post arrives at a house in Square Street on a bright sunny morning in October, 1956. Covent Garden Market, demolished about 1960, appears in the background.

postal traffic is colossal. Apart from packets the Leamington office now handles on average 345,000 letters (1st and 2nd class), per week. In the town there are 49 pillar and wall boxes and over 50 delivery rounds serve to bring the mail to the residents and businesses in the locality. Altogether there are 7 sub-post offices: Brunswick Street, Clarendon Street, Lillington, Kelvin Road, Milverton, Sydenham and Whitnash. The High Street sub-office closed August, 1981, while St. Mary's was transferred to Sydenham in March 1982. Since 1st September, 1986 outward 1st class mail from Leamington has been sent to the mechanised office at Bishop Street, Coventry, 2nd class mail having been already handled by Coventry for some time. This now means that the use of the Leamington and Warwick postmark has been discontinued.

The last Head Postmaster of Warwick and Leamington, Mr. Arthur Peat at a dinner dance for postal staff at the Spa Centre, 13th. December, 1980. During the evening, farewell presentations were made to Mr. Peat who was due to retire from the postal service on 31st. December.

In order to achieve much-needed cost savings, the British Post Office began over a number of years to investigate several schemes. One of those adopted was the concentration of administrative work followed by a regrading of Warwick and Leamington from a Head Postmastership to a Postmastership. The last Head Postmaster for Warwick and Leamington was Mr. Arthur Peat whose post at Leamington ceased on 17th September, 1978 and which he had occupied since 14th January, 1974. Mr. Peat left to take up duty as Assistant Postmaster at Coventry on 18th September. The post and title of Head Postmaster Warwick and Leamington did not actually cease until the 4th November 1978. The interim period, pending the regrading of the office, was covered by Mr. H. Renfree who was appointed Temporary Head Postmaster after which time the new title Postmaster was introduced. Further fundamental restructurings have created separate businesses for Royal Mail Letters, Royal Mail Parcels and Post Office Counters resulting in more local regradings.

Thus, after a period of just over 200 years the postal history of Leamington is brought up to date.

A view of Victoria Terrace, November 1980. It shows, to the left of traffic lights, the empty building previously used as a postal Branch Office from March 1971 until December 1978.

INDEX

(Illustrations denoted by italics or underlined page numbers)

Y

Yarningale Common 135
York Bridge 30, _82_
York Promenade *see* York Walk
York Road 28, 33
York Walk 30, 83